COLLEGE OF MARIN LIBRARY
KENTFIELD, CALIFORNIA

D0391943

BLOODHOUNDS
OF
HEAVEN

BLOODHOUNDS
OF
HEAVEN

The Detective in English Fiction
from Godwin to Doyle

Ian Ousby

Harvard University Press
Cambridge, Massachusetts, and London, England
1976

Copyright © 1976 by the President and Fellows of Harvard College
All rights reserved
Printed in the United States of America
Publication of this book has been aided by a grant from
   the Andrew W. Mellon Foundation.

Library of Congress Cataloging in Publication Data
Ousby, Ian, 1947–
   Bloodhounds of heaven.

   Includes bibliographical references and index.
   1. Detective and mystery stories, English—History
and criticism.   2. English fiction—19th century—
History and criticism.   3. Detectives in literature.
I. Title.
PR868.D409   823'.0872   76-7069
ISBN 0-674-07657-5

To my mother
and
to the memory of my father

Preface

Detective fiction is pre-eminently the literature of the sickroom and the railway carriage; even its admirers rarely argue that it is a serious art form. Nevertheless, it has attracted a surprising amount of serious commentary. E. M. Wrong, Willard Huntington Wright ("S. S. Van Dine"), and Dorothy L. Sayers all contributed pioneer essays during the middle and late 1920s, while the end of that decade saw the publication of Régis Messac's lengthy historical study, still the standard work in the field. Since then the list of secondary sources has steadily lengthened, and there are signs that a minor critical industry is coming to birth. In fact, since I began work on the present study in 1970, two short histories of detective fiction, Julian Symons' *Mortal Consequences* (English title: *Bloody Murder*) and Colin Watson's *Snobbery with Violence,* have appeared.

Inevitably, the student of the detective story is now confronted with an abundance of conflicting theories. The literary historians are divided into those, like Howard Haycraft, who see the genre as essentially a nineteenth century creation and hence stress the importance of Poe's contribution, and those, like Messac, who view it as an outgrowth of the puzzle tales so common in the literature of antiquity and in the fiction of the Enlightenment. Speculations about the source of the detective story's appeal are more diverse; indeed, enjoying the advantage of being virtually untestable, they sometimes verge on the exotic. Freud, for example, suggested that the genre recreates the infant's earliest sexual investigations, whereas Edmund Wilson thought its popularity, especially during the years between the two world wars, was founded on a pervasive sense of guilt characteristic of the modern consciousness. To most commentators the detective novel has seemed an expression of the modern belief in rational and scientific inquiry.

My study does not set out to be yet another history of detective fiction or yet another discussion of its aesthetics. It deals with the presentation of the detective himself, and discussion is confined to English fiction, beginning with William Godwin's *Caleb Williams* and concluding with Arthur Conan Doyle's Sherlock Holmes stories. It is thus a study of the creation, first of a literary hero, then of a series of literary stereotypes.

Although this subject has not been ignored by literary historians, the attention has usually been scant. Writers are correctly agreed that the main stages of the genre's development took place outside England: the nineteenth century tradition of the detective story began with Poe, continued with Gaboriau, and reached English literature only with the publication of Doyle's work near the end of the century. Victorian contributions—like Dickens' journalism about the police force and his unfinished novel *The Mystery of Edwin Drood*, or Wilkie Collins' *The Moonstone*—are usually mentioned by historians of detective fiction only in passing. Earlier works, such as *Caleb Williams*, commonly fare even worse.

This approach is justified if one's main interest is to sketch the prehistory of a form which did not reach maturity until the early years of the twentieth century. But as a picture of English nineteenth-century taste, it is profoundly misleading, for the age was fascinated by crime and its nemesis, by mysteries and their solution. This interest, however, was at once too loosely based and too serious to fit into the specialized and somewhat

Preface

rigid confines of the detective novel. It attached itself to a literary figure, the detective, rather than to a single literary genre.
My study therefore traces the detective through a variety of literary contexts; it deals with picaresque romances and sensation novels as well as with detective stories.

My discussion departs from critical orthodoxy in one important respect. Régis Messac's argument, now widely accepted,
is that the literary interest in detection can be explained
largely by reference to the growth of science and the popular-
ization of scientific method. But science and scientism did not
become relevant to the English portrayal of the detective until
the advent of Sherlock Holmes, and even then they were only
part of the picture. Before Holmes, English fictional detectives
were presented as criminal-catchers at least as much as puzzle-
solvers. A mildly salacious interest in crime or a more serious
interest in problems of public order predominated over any
concern with scientific methodology. The social history of the
period is therefore of peculiar relevance to the detective in literature: as my discussion will show, the history of the English
police force accounts for many significant developments in the
portrayal of the detective.

The importance of the social background renders my decision to concentrate on English fiction less arbitrary than it
might at first appear. Although the nineteenth century interest
in detection was an international phenomenon, local factors
could be vital in determining the forms that this interest took.
They help to explain, for example, the very different views of
the detective being offered at the same time in the fiction of
Dickens and of Balzac. Apart from passing references, my
study deals with foreign works only when they had a vital influence on English developments, and then they are discussed
primarily as influences rather than as works in their own
right. Thus, my account of Vidocq, the French detective,
centers on English reactions to his *Memoirs,* and consideration
of Poe's Dupin tales, written in the early 1840s, is deferred
until the chapter on Doyle, the first English writer whose view
of the detective Poe deeply affected.

Part of my second chapter appeared, in an earlier form, in
the *University of Toronto Quarterly.* I am grateful to the editors

of this journal and to University of Toronto Press for their permission to reprint. I am grateful also to John Murray Ltd. for permission to quote from *Sherlock Holmes: The Complete Short Stories* and *Sherlock Holmes: The Complete Long Stories* by Arthur Conan Doyle, and to Hutchinson and Co. Ltd. for permission to quote from *Thief-Taker General: The Rise and Fall of Jonathan Wild* by Gerald Howson. For my title I am indebted to a radio broadcast by the late C. Day Lewis, who used the phrase "bloodhound of heaven" to describe Georges Simenon's Inspector Maigret.

Many teachers, friends, and colleagues have helped in the making of this book. Professors Robert Kiely and Monroe Engel of Harvard University read the manuscript in its younger days as a doctoral dissertation; in its revised form it still bears evidence of their patience and knowledge. Professor Robert Lee Wolff of Harvard generously shared his exhaustive knowledge of Victorian fiction with me. My conversations with Professor Eamon Grennan of Vassar College were a constant source of stimulation. Virginia LaPlante of Harvard University Press has been at once the kindest and most rigorous of editors. I would also like to thank Anita Siskind for her great help in collecting illustrations. My greatest debt—it is too large for me to attempt to specify—is to my wife, Professor Heather Dubrow Ousby.

Contents

Illustrations

FROM ROGUERY TO RESPECTABILITY

DETECTION. *Means "taking the roof off," i.e., uncovering what is hidden. In the Spanish literary tradition, the Devil occasionally offered one of his favorites the entertainment of looking into all the houses of a town by taking the roofs off. Detectives are consequently sons or disciples of the Devil.*
     —Jacques Barzun and Wendell Hertig Taylor,
      A Catalogue of Crime

1

Thief-Taking
and Thief-Making

The relative positions of a police-officer and a professed thief bear a different complexion according to circumstances. The most obvious simile of a hawk pouncing upon his prey is often least acceptable. Sometimes the guardian of justice has the air of a cat watching a mouse, and, while he suspends his purpose of springing upon the pilferer, takes care so to calculate his motions that he shall not get beyond his power. Sometimes, more passive still, he uses the art of fascination ascribed to the rattlesnake, and contents himself with glaring on the victim through all his devious flutterings; certain that his terror, confusion, and disorder of ideas will bring him into his jaws at last. The interview between Ratcliffe and Sharpitlaw had an aspect different from all these. They sate for five minutes silent, on opposite sides of a small table, and looked fixedly at each other, with a sharp, knowing, and alert cast of countenance, not unmingled with an inclination to laugh, and resembled more than anything else two dogs who, preparing for a game of romps, are seen to couch down and remain in that posture for a little time, watching each other's movements, and waiting which shall begin the game.[1]

To Sir Walter Scott the phrase "cops and robbers" would not have suggested a simple and satisfying moral dichotomy. Describing the relationship between the lawman and the criminal in *The Heart of Midlothian*, he turned, like so many writers of his age, to the simile of the hunt and imagery of the animal world. If the parallel with a beast of prey endows the policeman or detective with suggestions of impressive power and skill, it also makes him a disturbing and suspect figure. Rather than appearing the embodiment of society's belief in justice and order, he belongs to an alien world, uncivilized, amoral, and potentially savage. He seems, in fact, far closer in spirit to the criminal than to the average citizen. Fittingly enough, Scott concludes with the meeting of Sharpitlaw and Ratcliffe, "dogs" both, deuteragonists in an occult ritual incomprehensible to the law-abiding spectator.

Such suspicions of the detective were hardly unique to the country and period in which Scott wrote; indeed, they can be seen in contemporary America, where they have encouraged the growth of the "hard-boiled" school of detective fiction. Yet they were of peculiar importance to English society in the early nineteenth century, caused by a complex of factors originating in the history of the preceding century. Sir Robert Peel's creation of the "New Police" in 1829 was to pave the way for the acceptance of both policemen and detectives which still characterizes English society. Before that date, however, the older system and the attitudes which perpetuated it had established a sharply defined and unfavorable public image of the detective, one which was to dominate his early characterization in fiction.

The eighteenth century believed that the law should be severe and that it should be seen to be severe. Capital offenses were added to the criminal law with a frequency which earned it the nickname of the Bloody Code, while executions were public, frequent, and popular. Yet, while the legislature stressed severity of punishment and sought to impress that severity on the public mind, it neglected the role of law enforcement. Convicted criminals suffered the heaviest of penalties, but the system offered relatively little assurance that criminals would actually be caught or detected. By modern standards England was, in Patrick Pringle's phrase, a "policeless state."[2]

The system that did exist was characterized by a belief in the amateur and by the amateurish nature of its operations. Its basic administrative unit was the parish, and its main functionaries were the justice of the peace and the parish constable. The justice of the peace was both the parish's magistrate and its chief of police; the post was voluntary and unpaid, but carried with it a certain social prestige. The local constable assisted the justice of the peace in police work; the office was a compulsory duty rotated among local property-owners, like modern jury service. Since the post of constable was unpaid and unprestigious, its holders tended increasingly to delegate the work to hired substitutes.

In London, where the pressure from a rising crime rate and frequent public disorders was greater than in rural areas, the system achieved a baroque complexity but no greater coherence or effectiveness. Here the constable was supplemented by the local nightly watch, whose existence dated back to the late seventeenth century. The "Charlies," as the watch were popularly known, might seem to have represented a creeping professionalism, for they received a salary. The wage, however, was a mere retaining fee, and the job became a sinecure for the old, the infirm, and the corrupt. In addition, local and privately organized police forces—rudimentary patrols or bands of vigilantes—sprang up to meet a particular problem or a particular panic. In 1828, the year before Peel's reforms, the responsibility for law enforcement in London remained divided among some seventy authorities, "a tangle of independent establishments" lacking both central control and the willingness to co-operate.[3]

The rudimentary and ineffective nature of the system is reflected in the public images of its agents. The "trading justice," or corrupt magistrate, was a familiar figure, epitomized by Henry Fielding's Mr. Thrasher in *Amelia:*

> if he was ignorant of the laws of England, [he] was yet well versed in the laws of nature. He perfectly well understood that fundamental principle so strongly laid down in the institutes of the learned Rochefoucault, by which the duty of self-love is so strongly enforced, and every man is taught to consider himself as the centre of gravity, and to attract all things thither. To speak the truth plainly, the justice was never indifferent in a cause but when he could get nothing on either side.[4]

Similarly, the members of the watch passed into folk memory as worthy descendants of Shakespeare's Dogberry and Verges:

> those poor old decrepit people who are, from their want of bodily strength, rendered incapable of getting a livelihood by work. These men, armed only with a pole, which some of them are scarce able to lift, are to secure the persons and houses of his Majesty's subjects from the attacks of gangs of young, bold, stout, desperate, and well-armed villains . . . If the poor old fellows should run away from such enemies, no one I think can wonder, unless it be that they were able to make their escape.[5]

It was inevitable that "knocking down Charlies" should have seemed to Pierce Egan's Tom and Jerry a fitting way to round off one of their nightly rambles and sprees through the metropolis.

There were, however, signs of change. At Bow Street Henry

and John Fielding approached their work as magistrates with a belief in the importance of police organization and introduced a number of reforms. They established patrols designed to bring a measure of security to the dangerously insecure streets of London, an information service about robberies and wanted men, and a small detective force, the Bow Street Runners.

The formation of the Runners was an attempt to introduce a measure of professionalism into the business of criminal investigation. They worked under the direction of the magistrates, received a small salary, which in 1797 was eleven shillings and sixpence a week, in 1821 twenty-five shillings, and enjoyed unlimited jurisdiction.[6] This freedom to range across the parish boundaries that normally hampered police activity was a considerable advantage: on occasion the Runners traveled throughout England, and even abroad, in pursuit of a particular individual. The advantages of the Fieldings' reforms in this and other areas were officially recognized in 1792, when the Middlesex Justices Act created seven new police offices in London on the Bow Street model. The runners at these offices, however, lacked unlimited jurisdiction, and they never achieved the fame and prestige of their Bow Street colleagues.

The preceding year saw the creation of an effective system for checking crime in the Port of London, the Marine Police Establishment, subsumed two years later into the Thames River Police. Such reforms, however, were necessarily piecemeal, out of temper with the spirit of the age, and limited in effect. Despite the obvious need for reform, and despite frequent consideration of the subject by parliamentary committees, the system remained substantially unchanged until the Metropolitan Police Act of 1829.

The system's persistence was not merely the result of oversight or of a tendency to stress severity of punishment in dealing with crime. The English, as reformers were given to lamenting, were traditionally prejudiced against the idea of a police force. Effective police arrangements would inevitably involve additional taxation, whereas the existing system had at least the virtue of cheapness. Improved operations would depend on centralized control, a concept to which the English—believers in parochial administration—were hostile in all areas of bureaucracy. Moreover, the idea of a uniformed and state-controlled police force evoked disturbing memories of the standing armies of Stuart and Cromwellian times. This tendency to associate the police with the army and hence with political tyranny, a vital impediment to reform for many years, was strengthened by the example of France. The gendarme's very name recalled his military origin, while his preoccupation with political security as well as with crime was a byword: "The Police of Foreigners," Sir John Fielding wrote, "is chiefly employed, and at an immense Expence, to enquire into and discover the common and indifferent Transactions of innocent Inhabitants and of harmless Travellers, which regard themselves only, and but faintly relate to the Peace of Society; this Policy may be useful in arbitrary Governments, but here it would be contemptible, therefore both useless and impracticable." [7]

The English were thus in the happy position of being able to resist a possible innovation on the grounds that it was expensive, tyrannical, and foreign. At times, the aversion to police even appeared to be greater than the aversion to crime. A foreign observer, who despite his irony did not share the prejudice, reported that "the English will have no such establishment (as that set up in France); they are afraid of troops, and . . . had rather be robb'd upon the highways than in their houses, and by wretches of desperate fortune than by ministers." [8]

Yet criminals had to be caught and Tyburn be kept busy. As the list of capital offenses was steadily extended throughout the eighteenth century, the methods by which the law was enforced were also gradually supplemented. The process was not the enactment of a predetermined policy but rather the application of a series of *ad hoc* measures which became first habitual and finally traditional. Suspicious of bureaucratic organization and hostile to the notion of a modern police force, legislators came to place responsibility for the detection of crime in the hands of private interest rather than public service. The system they created, as Leon Radzinowicz has written, "was largely inspired by the creed of *laissez-faire* and to an appreciable extent was worked by private initiative, principles which were so natural to the Englishman's way of life and thought." [9]

In essence the new system depended on a number of "temptations and threats" designed to encourage the average citizen, the police officer, and the criminal himself to detect and prosecute crime. Criminals were offered pardons for betraying their accomplices, while police officers could be fined for failing to carry out their duties. On the capture and conviction of a criminal, the citizen responsible could claim a "Tyburn ticket," an exemption from certain parish duties.

The two most important developments were an increased reliance on the informer and the growth of a system of financial rewards. The common informer reported and prosecuted various infringements of the law in order to obtain a share of the fine imposed by the court. His existence dated back several centuries, but in the eighteenth century he acquired new importance. Various statutes provided him with the incentive to prosecute a wide variety of minor criminals, such as offenders against gambling laws and laws concerning weights and measures. With this increased field of activity, the informer became to contemporaries a familiar figure.

The exploitation of the profit motive was at its most apparent in the rewards system. The so-called Highwayman Act of 1692 offered a "parliamentary reward" of forty pounds to any individual who captured and successfully prosecuted a highwayman. During the course of the following century the practice was extended, and amounts varying from ten to forty pounds were paid for the prosecution of a large number of crimes against property, in cases where the offence was "accompanied by aggravating circumstances . . . of frequent occurrence, easy to commit, but difficult to detect."[10] When this measure by itself proved inadequate, it was supplemented by specially advertised rewards. The government itself, local authorities, special societies, and aggrieved parties all offered surprisingly large amounts of money for the prosecution of particular offenses or particular individuals.

Both public officials and private citizens could claim rewards or shares in fines. The system was designed both to increase the parish constable's dangerously small incentive for doing his duty and to create an additional force of free-lance policemen. The eighteenth century detective could thus be either an officer of the peace or a self-employed private citizen, and he was paid solely by results.

Jeremy Bentham, that caustic critic of the anomalies of English law, noted a paradox in its attitude to informers and "thief-takers," as reward-hunters were called: "It employs them, oftentimes deceives them, and always holds them up to contempt."[11] Though the system itself was almost unanimously supported, its agents became the objects of continual public opprobrium. Henry Fielding complained: "So far are men from being animated with the hopes of public praise to apprehend a felon, that they are even discouraged by the fear of shame. The person of the informer is in fact more odious than that of the felon himself; and the thief-catcher is in danger of worse treatment from the populace than the thief."[12] After the passage of the Gin Act in 1736, which relied heavily on informers for its enforcement, the public, in the words of a contemporary, "now began to declare war against [informers] . . . many of whom they treated with great cruelty and some they murdered in the streets."[13] Two years later it was necessary to pass a law making assault on an informer punishable by seven years' transportation, but the hostility and the occasional violence persisted. The thief-takers enjoyed a similar fate at the hands of public opinion. The rewards for which they worked quickly became known as "blood money." Sir John Fielding refused to reveal the names of his early Runners at Bow Street for their own protection, "as the thief-takers are extremely obnoxious to the common people."[14]

The grounds for this hostility were simple. Already unsympathetic to police measures, the English public found in addition that men who sought out their neighbors' petty offenses or who sent criminals to the gallows for cash offended against elementary notions of honor and honesty. The system had attempted to secure efficient detection of crime by appealing to the motives "that govern the actions of mankind."[15] In practice, however, it was apparent that the system appealed more widely to the dishonest than the honest. Peace officers apart, few citizens were in a position to profit from the offer of rewards. The necessary information and the necessary skills belonged more naturally to criminals and their associates. Like the offer of pardons, the rewards system was mainly successful in persuading thieves to turn against their fellows. "However lamentable it is to think that Magistrates are compelled to have recourse to such expedients," wrote Patrick Colquhoun, himself a distinguished magistrate, "yet while the present system continues, and while robberies and burglaries are so frequent, without the means of prevention, there is no alternative on many occasions *but to employ a thief to catch a thief.*" [16] Though the necessity for such measures might be conceded, their agents—men like Scott's Ratcliffe—inevitably appeared to be merely canny and self-interested traitors to their own kind.

It became progressively clearer that the system contained open invitations to corruption. By turning thief-taker, the thief did not necessarily contribute to justice and public order. As Radzinowicz has noted, "the temptation which the rewards offered to the cupidity of police officers and others was so strong that ultimately [they] . . . proved almost as much a source of crime as a stimulus to its detection." [17] The fact that the amount of the reward increased with the seriousness of the offense encouraged the thief-taker not to apprehend the petty criminal but to wait until he committed a more serious crime. "Criminals were permitted to ripen from the first stage of depravity until they were worth forty pounds," Colquhoun complained, ". . . which subjected the Public to the intermediate depredations of every villain from his first starting, till he could be clearly convicted to a capital offence." [18] In the eyes of the thief-taker the criminal underworld was a harvest, permitted to grow until the financial incentive for reaping became sufficiently great.

In addition, the fact that the thief-taker was paid for the conviction rather than the arrest of the criminal encouraged perjury. As a chief prosecution witness, he had a direct financial interest in persuading the court to return a verdict of "guilty." Testifying before a parliamentary committee in 1816, John Townshend, a Bow Street Runner, spoke wryly and surprisingly frankly to this point: "I for one should naturally say, if placed upon the Jury, yes, it may be true these officers are speaking the truth; but it turns out by cross-examination that there is £120 to be given if these three men are convicted, and therefore I cannot believe all these men have sworn." [19]

Spectacular examples of corruption amongst thief-takers were not wanting. In the years 1754–1759 public attention was first drawn to the existence of conspiracies to obtain blood money by the trials of the thief-taker Stephen MacDaniel and his gang. In 1816 the trial of several Bow Street officers for conspiracy again drew attention to the "horrible trade in blood demands," as the *Times* called it, and here the public reaction was all the stronger since the accused men were not self-employed thief-takers but official public servants.[20] "The true extent of the evil will never be known," Leon Radzinowicz has concluded. "If some conspiracies were discovered, many more remained undetected."[21]

The MacDaniel conspiracy was brought to light by Joseph Cox, High Constable of the hundred of Blackheath, one of "the handful of peace officers who were not only efficient but acted out of their historical context by voluntarily doing work for the public good without any prospect of private gain."[22] Cox's investigations, a model of careful and intelligent detection, uncovered a simple pattern. MacDaniel and his confederates had decoyed two youths, Kelly and Ellis, into committing a staged robbery. They then arrested the youths and, together with the "victim" of the robbery, gave evidence designed to secure the reward for their conviction. Further investigation by Cox revealed an earlier conspiracy in which Joshua Kidden, apparently a completely innocent man, had been hanged on MacDaniel's evidence.

The subsequent trials of the conspirators showed the paradoxical nature of the age's attitude to thief-takers. Indictments for being accessories before the fact to robbery, for conspiring to defeat public justice, and for murdering Kidden all failed, despite Cox's most diligent efforts. After several trials the thief-takers were convicted and sentenced for only one non-capital offense: malicious conspiracy to obtain the convictions of Ellis and Kelly. Reluctance to sustain the graver charges was based, as Blackstone discreetly put it, on "prudential reasons."[23] The legislature was committed to the use of rewards to induce people to give evidence against criminals, so it hesitated to "counter this with the deterring thought that evidence might be at the peril of the witness's life."[24] Yet while the final result of the trials underlined the official commitment to the thief-taking system, public hatred of the thief-takers themselves asserted itself. In his pamphlet on the case, Cox described the fate of MacDaniel and his three confederates after their conviction for malicious conspiracy:

Pursuant to their Sentence, Macdaniel and Berry, on the 5th of March, stood in the Pillory in Holborn near Hatton-Garden, and were so severely handled by the Populace, that it was with the utmost Difficulty that one of the Sheriffs and the Keeper of Newgate, who stood in a Balcony just by, prevented their being utterly destroyed; and so great was the Mob, that the Peace-Officers found it impossible to protect the Prisoners from their Fury.

March 8, Gahagan and Salmon stood in the Pillory in the Middle of Smithfield-Rounds; they were instantly assaulted with Showers of Oyster-shells, Stones, &c. and had not stood above half an Hour before Gahagan was struck dead, and Salmon was so dangerously wounded in the Head, that it was thought impossible he could recover.[25]

To the eighteenth century public the thief-taker could seem as disturbing a figure as the criminal himself. Indeed, the two appeared more than a little similar: often drawn from the same sector of society, they both served motives of crude self-interest and could both show a chilling disregard for the elementary rules of ethical conduct. The suspicion that the thief-taker and the criminal were blood-brothers rather than enemies received its most striking confirmation in the career of Jonathan Wild. To contemporaries Wild's life was a *cause célèbre*, the subject for widespread popular debate, for ballads and pamphlets, and for political satire. For future generations it became a folk legend which established the detective as a figure of malignant power.

Today Wild is chiefly remembered as the hero of Fielding's novel *Jonathan Wild*. In fact, the novelist's insistence on Wild's "greatness" is more than a literary embellishment and has a truth beyond the realm of satire. As Gerald Howson has suggested in his biography of Wild, the thief-taker possessed "an abundance of what the eighteenth century called 'Genius'— that is, ingenuity, cunning, resource, energy and that mysterious power we sometimes call 'personal magnetism.'"[26] At times, his career seems like a grim real-life version of one of the age's picaresque novels: an energetic and bloodthirsty progression from rags to riches to Tyburn.

Born in 1683 at Wolverhampton, Wild came to London in his

youth. After a spell in a debtors' prison he became assistant to Charles Hitchen, the Under City-Marshal. One of the most corrupt law enforcers in an age notorious for its corruption, Hitchen found in Wild an apt pupil. By 1714 Wild had left Hitchen's employment and set up in business by himself. The business was bound to prove attractive to the citizens of London. With the official enforcers of the law continually demonstrating their inadequacy, Wild offered to recover stolen goods for a discreet fee. His system proved effective, and the reputation of his "Lost Property Office" quickly spread. Daniel Defoe later wrote: "He was now Master of his Trade, Poor and Rich flock'd to him: If any Thing was Lost, (Whether by Negligence in the Owner, or Vigilance and Dexterity in the Thief) away we went to *Jonathan Wild*. Nay, Advertisements were Publish'd directing the Finder of almost every Thing, to bring it to *Jonathan Wild*, who was eminently impower'd to take it, and give the Reward."[27] Defoe himself consulted Wild about the loss of a silver-hilted sword. The theft seems to have been too trifling to engage the great man's full attention, and Defoe never got his sword back. Nevertheless, his account of the incident conveys the air of businesslike efficiency which Wild radiated:

I REMEMBER I had occasion, in a Case of this Kind, to wait upon Mr. *Jonathan* with a Crown in my Hand . . . and having made a Deposite, I was ask'd . . . where the Thing was lost? At first he smil'd, and turning to one, I suppose of his Instruments, who can this be? says he, why all our People are gone down to *Sturbridge* Fair; the other answer'd, after some pause, I think I saw *Lynx*, in the Street, Yesterday: Did you, says he, then 'tis that Dog, I warrant you. Well, Sir, says he, I believe we can find out your Man; you shall know more of it, if you let me see you again a *Monday*.[28]

Appearing thus in the role of public servant, Wild added to his reputation by his activities as a thief-taker. He himself claimed to have been responsible for the arrest of seventy-five criminals, but Howson has suggested that the full list of Wild's captures would in fact be even longer: "a total of 120 or even 150 would seem quite reasonable."[29] As a thief-taker, he was energetic, skillful, and courageous; and he was supported by an impressive network of agents, a crude private detective force. In 1716 he captured the five men who had robbed and murdered a Mrs. Knap. Both the crime and Wild's success attracted notice, and Wild received rewards totaling £270 (about £5,400 or $13,500 in modern terms).[30] In the early 1720s he broke up several of London's most notorious gangs, and in 1724 he achieved his most famous capture. Jack Sheppard and his accomplice, Blueskin Blake, were tried for robbery and—after Sheppard's several escapes from prison—hanged at Tyburn.

"A Lawyer is an honest employment, so is mine," reflects Peachum, Wild's literary counterpart in John Gay's *The Beggar's Opera*. "Like me too he acts in a double capacity, both against Rogues and for 'em; for 'tis but fitting that we should protect and encourage Cheats, since we live by 'em."[31] Rather than being the scourge of the underworld—"The Thief-Taker General of Great Britain and Ireland," as Wild flamboyantly styled himself—Wild was in fact its most powerful member. The robberies he "investigated" took place under his own supervision and protection. In addition, he was involved in a host of other criminal activities. In him, Howson has argued, modern organized crime found its pioneer:

> Certainly he resembled the gangster of the twentieth century more closely than he did his famous contemporaries in Europe, such as "Cartouche," who were simply robber-chieftains in the old tradition. He was the first criminal to become a "celebrity" known to everyone in Town, a good neighbour, a prominent citizen who petitioned for the Freedom of London, and a donator to charitable causes; the first to keep books like an accountant and to understand that crime is a business, and that it needs the same care, attention and planning that all businesses need if they are not to fail; the first to employ respectable lawyers on permanent retainer in order to outwit the courts with their own jargon; and the first, a quality much admired at the time, to use "science" in the art of detection. Like his successors today, he never dropped the mask of respectability, although, unlike many of them, he was humorous enough to wear it sometimes in a spirit of self-mockery.[32]

In Wild's case the detective was not merely corrupt or similar to the criminal in his methods: he was also a master criminal. The two professions, moreover, were not merely alternative sources of income, but necessary complements. Wild's Lost Property Office was the means by which he disposed of the goods stolen by gangs under his supervision. Similarly, according to Howson, his work as a thief-taker consolidated and increased his power over the underworld: "the hundreds of criminals he . . . 'brought to Justice' were casualties or 'fall guys' to use the best expression, in a dark and hidden gang-warfare waged against enemies, rivals, and 'rebels.' "[33] Such rackets were not new, and they did not die with him, yet Wild pursued his double career with an "Impudence & shameless Boldness," a cunning and flair, that gave him no real predecessors or successors.[34]

In 1725 Wild was arrested for receiving stolen goods under an Act of Parliament passed some years earlier and popularly known as the Jonathan Wild Act. With the exposure of his crimes he became the focus of public attention, and his trial and execution at Tyburn called forth a small hailstorm of pamphlets and "true accounts." To the satirists of the age he came as a godsend. In *The Beggar's Opera* written in 1727 and in Fielding's novel written some years later, his life became the epitome of the corruptions of society, a low-life equivalent of the trickery of statesmen and politicians.

To a society faced with innumerable problems of crime and law enforcement, the case had a more practical bearing. A number of contemporaries were ready to tolerate Wild as a necessary evil, for the same reason that the judiciary had been unwilling to condemn MacDaniel and his gang. After Wild had been attacked in court by one of his victims, Blueskin Blake, a ballad-writer (possibly Jonathan Swift) prematurely celebrated Wild's death with an invocation to the underworld: "Now *Blueskin's* sharp Penknife has set you at Ease,/ and ev'ry Man round me may rob if he please."[35] The belief that Wild had prevented crime survived his exposure and execution. A rise in the crime rate was blamed on his absence, and a foreign visitor reported that many Englishmen felt that "more harm was done than good by the execution of this famous thief, for there is now no one to go to who will help you recover your stolen property; the government has certainly got rid of a robber, but he was only one, whereas by his help several were hanged every year."[36]

Wild could be defended as useful, and even glorified enough for Fielding to feel that the legend needed debunking. Yet in general the case served to crystallize the suspicions of the thief-taker and detective. The public reaction to the scandal was all the stronger for its anger at having been gulled. Jack Sheppard had died, as notorious criminals often did, amidst the applause and sympathy of the crowd. The scene at Wild's death, on the contrary, as Defoe described it, was very like the punishment of MacDaniel and his colleagues:

> here was nothing to be heard but Cursings and Execrations; abhorring the Crimes and the very Name of the Man, throwing Stones and Dirt at him all the way, and even at the Place of Execution; the other Malefactors being all ready to be turn'd off, but the Hangman giving him leave to take his own Time, and he continuing setting down in the Cart, the Mob impatient, and fearing a Reprieve, tho' they had no occasion for it, call'd furiously upon the Hangman to dispatch him, and at last threatened to tear him to pieces, if he did not tye him up immediately.
>
> IN short there was a kind of an universal Rage against him, which nothing but his Death could satisfie or put an end to.[37]

Defoe's account of Wild's life echoes the sentiments of the mob at Tyburn. Lamenting the tendency of other writers to "make a Jest of his Story," Defoe proceeds to sketch Wild's career as the tragedy of a man of a "pushing, enterprizing Nature" who brought about his downfall by overreaching ambition. Its hero was "a Man turn'd into an incarnate Devil, his Life a Scene of inimitable Crimes; his very Society a Hell, and equally devouring both to Soul and Body."[38] The allusion to the devil is intentional, for Wild, according to Defoe, performed the traditionally demonic role of temptation and destruction:

> BUT which is still worse than all the rest, I have several Stories by me at this Time, which I have particular Reason to believe are true, of Children thus strolling about the

Streets in Misery and Poverty, whom he has taken in on
pretence of providing for them, and employing them; and
all has ended in this (*viz.*) making Rogues of them. *Horrid
Wickedness!* his Charity has been to breed them up to be
Thieves, and *still more horrid!* several of these his own
forster Children, he has himself caused afterwards to be
apprehended and Hang'd for the very Crimes which he
first taught them how to Commit.[39]

The spectacle of Wild's villainy produced no serious evalua-
tion of the system that had made it possible, but Wild himself
was not quickly forgotten. As late as 1899 a popular writer
about crime and detection could consider his story "sufficiently well known" to need little rehearsal.[40] Like Macchia-
velli and Napoleon, Wild earned a place in folk memory as a
symbol of incarnate evil. The popular view is exemplified by
Harrison Ainsworth's immensely successful novel *Jack Sheppard* (1839), itself the progenitor of a number of nineteenth
century melodramas. Here Wild plays an almost archetypal
role, an elaboration of Defoe's portrait. Fagin-like, the thief-
taker lures the likable and adventurous young Sheppard into a
life of crime and, finally, to a martyr's death at Tyburn. Wild
is, as he himself proudly declares, the "evil genius" of the
piece.[41]

Out of the confusions and complexities of the eighteenth
century system of law enforcement the detective emerges as a
figure of proportions alien and surprising to the modern mind.
Associated with corruption and dishonesty, he appears strikingly similar to the criminal himself. In the legend of Jonathan
Wild this unfavorable picture takes on a sharper and more extreme form: a devil-figure and bogey man, simultaneously
both detective and criminal. Impressed deeply on the public
mind, this view of the detective inevitably influenced his portrayal in literature. He entered fiction not as a hero, but as, at
worst, a villain and, at best, a suspect and ambiguous character.

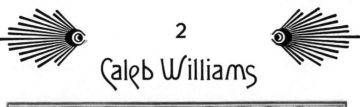

2
Caleb Williams

Published in 1794, William Godwin's *Caleb Williams* was conceived, in the words of its original subtitle, as an examination of "Things as They Are." It offered a radical analysis of existing society, finding in the operations of the criminal law the epitome of an omnipresent tyranny. Thus, it was almost inevitable that the book should include a portrait of a thief-taker. Gines, the thief-taker who acts as the principal agent of the villain Falkland in his pursuit and persecution of the hero Caleb, is clearly intended as a representative of his profession. Like many of his counterparts in real life, he "fluctuated . . . between the two professions of a violator of the laws and a retainer to their administration. He had originally devoted himself to the first, and probably his initiation in the mysteries of thieving qualified him to be peculiarly expert in the profession of a thief-taker" (259–260).[1]

Even Gines himself takes a low view of thief-taking: he adopts it "not from choice, but necessity" and is "intimately persuaded that there was no comparison between the liberal and manly profession of robber . . . and the sordid and mechanical occupation of a bloodhunter" (260–261). The narrative rejects Gines's view of robbery but bears out his view of thief-taking. On his first appearance, the thief-taker robs and assaults Caleb. The incident serves to enforce both the reader's and the hero's newly acquired sense of man's inhumanity to man. Thereafter Gines develops into the clearest example of one of Godwin's main preoccupations, the savage jungle animal lurking inside civilized man. The thief-taker's pursuit of Caleb is everywhere shown to be an act of greed and rapacity.

The novel, however, is noteworthy for more than its succinct vignette of a typical thief-taker, drawn in the light of contemporary attitudes. *Caleb Williams* is the first work of English fiction to display a sustained interest in the theme of detection. Literary historians have been quick to note this fact, but their accounts have usually stressed Godwin's contribution to the structure of later detective fiction, his careful planning, and his attempt to achieve "an entire unity of plot" (337).[2] The portrait of Caleb Williams himself, though commonly overlooked, is no less significant.

In fact, Caleb is the first important detective in the English novel. As a young man, he enters the service of the local

Caleb Williams

squire, Falkland, and falls unintentionally and unthinkingly into the role of spy on his master. Falkland seems a walking enigma: previously a polished and elegant man of the world, he has recently retired into gloomy solitude. Upon inquiry Caleb learns about the origins of Falkland's depression from Mr. Collins, the steward of the manor. When Tyrrel, a boorish neighbor with whom Falkland had publicly quarreled, was murdered, suspicion had naturally fallen on Falkland. Even though he was quickly vindicated, Falkland apparently found this slight upon his reputation a permanent source of shame. Dissatisfied with this explanation, Caleb cultivates his master's company and becomes adroit at discreet interrogation. He finally learns that Falkland's secret is darker than had been supposed: Falkland is really Tyrrel's murderer.

In a tart and witty essay on *Caleb Williams* Thomas De Quincey concluded that its hero's detection is really a "vile eavesdropping inquisitiveness."[3] He offered the judgment as something of a *jeu d'esprit,* but it contains an important element of truth for, despite Caleb's obvious courage, energy, and resourcefulness, the reader's view of his character is ultimately hostile. His detective activities involve, in a subtler and transmuted form, several of the themes associated with both Gines and his real-life counterparts. The characterization of Caleb thus shows how the sociologically determined suspicions of the detective manifest themselves in a complex fictional context.

In modern detective fiction the detective plays a role like that of the Duke in Shakespearean comedy: a moral hero and a figure of power, he establishes intellectual certainties and restores the order which has previously been threatened. Caleb Williams, on the contrary, is essentially a tragic figure, powerless in everything except his ability to catalyze discord. His discovery of Falkland's guilt does little good and a great deal of harm. Caleb lacks both the concrete evidence and the inclination to accuse his master publicly. Yet, for his part, Falkland is sufficiently alarmed at the discovery of his secret to turn the tables on the detective. He accuses Caleb of stealing valuables from the house and manages to get him imprisoned. Even after his escape from prison, Caleb is not safe from his ex-master's power; Falkland and his agent Gines dog the hero's foot-

steps, blackening his reputation wherever he goes. At the end
of the book Caleb is finally goaded into a public accusation of
Falkland. A court believes the charge and Falkland dies of grief
at seeing his good name destroyed.

Even though Caleb is finally successful, the import of the
denouement is profoundly dissimilar from its equivalents in
modern detective fiction. Superficially a moment of triumph
for the detective, it is really a moment of psychological and
moral defeat. It destroys even the detective's certainties about
himself. Caleb ends by confessing: "I thought that, if Falkland
were dead, I should return once again to all that makes life
worth possessing. I thought that, if the guilt of Falkland were
established, fortune and the world would smile upon my efforts. Both these events are accomplished; and it is only now
that I am truly miserable" (325).

In deciding to write a tragic novel, Godwin was obviously
aware of the precedent set some fifty years earlier by Samuel
Richardson's *Clarissa*. He himself recorded that, as he composed *Caleb Williams*, "it was ever [his] method to get about
[him] any productions of former authors that seemed to bear
on [his] subject" (339). Despite so scholarly a concern for previous work in his field, Godwin was also open to literary influences of a deeper, less studied sort. He remarked that he
"amused [himself] with tracing a certain similitude between
the story of Caleb Williams and the tale of Bluebeard" (340). In
the light of such a remark, one must seek beyond Richardson
for precedents for the book's tragic movement, and an important analogue is found in Renaissance and Jacobean revenge
tragedy.[4] According to this analogy, the detective, the victim
of the tragic process, is similar not to the Richardsonian model
of saintly innocence but to the morally ambiguous figure of the
revenger.

At the beginning of the novel Caleb, as he also remarks elsewhere, is "raw and inexperienced" (282). Brought up as the
son of "humble parents in a remote county of England" (3), he
had spent his youth in a single and limited sector of society.
He is clearly no simple hayseed, but his view of life and his
knowledge of the world smack distinctly of the evening class
and the midnight oil; they are bookish and theoretical rather
than experiential. "Though I was not a stranger to books," he

explains to the reader, "I had no practical acquaintance with men" (5).

His move from the village to Falkland's manor house involves him for the first time in a world of experience and complexity. In contrast to the world of Caleb's youth, Falkland's world is one of social power and sophistication, of intellectual and cultural refinement. Through his acquaintance with Falkland and his detective investigations, Caleb is introduced to psychological and moral complexities for which neither village life nor his books had prepared him. Mr. Collins' narrative of Falkland's past life comes as an exciting but alarming revelation to Caleb:

> Hitherto I had had no intercourse with the world and its passions; and, though I was not totally unacquainted with them as they appear in books, this proved to be of little service to me when I came to witness them myself. The case seemed entirely altered, when the subject of those passions was continually before my eyes, and the events had happened but the other day as it were, in the very neighbourhood where I lived. There was a connection and progress in this narrative, which made it altogether unlike the little village incidents I had hitherto known. (106)

The hero of revenge tragedy undergoes a similar development. Like Caleb, Hamlet and Vindice are scholars thrust into a world of action, a world of decisions with direct human consequences rather than of abstract problems. Again like Caleb, Bussy D'Ambois is the blunt countryman forced to cope with the complexities of court life. In both literal and symbolic terms the court of Jacobean drama and Falkland's manor house function similarly: they epitomize the world of sophistication and complexity with which the hero must deal. Moreover, the complexities presented to Caleb by Falkland's life assume a form familiar in revenge tragedy: the hidden crime or sin which gives the lie to the avowed public standards of morality.

In these circumstances the reaction of the revenge hero is a delicate balance of attraction and repulsion. He becomes a railer at corruption, fascinated by what he attacks. Caleb's reaction to Falkland hinges on a similar paradox. Initially viewing his master as an unspotted emblem of innocence and purity, he then deliberately destroys this ideal image by embarking on his detective activities. Once Caleb has discovered the truth about Falkland's murder of Tyrrel, he oscillates between continued admiration and a hatred of both Falkland and the social system he represents. To be sure, Caleb's polemics against "the whole machine of society" (183) are for the most part pallid set-pieces, and the reader quickly senses that the hero is merely a convenient mouthpiece for the radical author. On occasion, however, the disembodied rhetoric gives way to dramatic urgency and an intensity of image; it takes on accents closer to the misanthropic disgust of the malcontent than to the measured analysis of Godwin's *Political Justice*, as in Caleb's remark, "I regarded the whole human species as so many hangmen and torturers" (183).

Caleb's curiosity, the motive that makes him turn detective, corresponds to the revenger's desire for revenge. In Jacobean drama revenge has an awkward habit of recoiling upon its actor's head, and the revenger commonly dies hoist with his own petard. Caleb's detection exposes him to the same fate. With his discovery of Falkland's crime Caleb's role—to use his own terminology—switches from the "offensive" to the "defensive" (134). Successful as a detective, he almost immediately finds himself in the dock rather than the witness box, and thereafter moves steadily toward social disgrace and psychological ruin. The stages of his destruction mirror his activities as a detective. Having tampered with his master's trunk in an attempt to find evidence about Tyrrel's murder, he finds stolen goods planted in his own trunks. Having threatened his master's reputation and acted as his inquisitor, he finds his own good name destroyed and his life subject to the terrible "vigilance of tyranny" (3).[5]

The revenger's fate as victim of his own machinations represents a judgment on his actions. As the dying Laertes sees, his death is an ironic stroke of justice. For revenge in Jacobean drama is a morally corrosive activity. Superficially it appears to make its actor the agent of justice; yet far from exemplifying his moral integrity, it calls into question and impairs that integrity. Corrupted by the pursuit of revenge, the revenger dies a victim of the disease he has begun by attempting to cure. Yet viewing a similar reversal in his own life, Caleb Williams can see only a grim irony of fate and an indictment of the social system. His resemblance to the revenger is completed by a nuance which eludes him: the element of punishment, of implicit judgment on the questionable morality of his own activities as a detective.

Caleb Williams, then, can be viewed as a modernized version of the revenge tragedy. The parallel serves to underline the book's essential movement and to suggest the terms by which its hero should be judged. Like the revenger, Caleb in his role as detective is subject to criticism for both his morals and his motives. The matter is complicated, however, by the fact that the entire story is told by Caleb himself: as an autobiographer, he is bent on self-vindication, not self-criticism. He distracts attention from his failings by describing his character in deceptively simple and laudatory terms. According to his own acccount, he is merely innocent and curious.

Caleb's protestations of innocence begin on the book's first page. "My own conscience," he declares, "witnesses in behalf of that innocence my pretensions to which are regarded in the world as incredible" (3). Indeed, he has undertaken the narrative to clear himself of the charge of theft which Falkland has used to blacken his character and render his adult life "a theatre of calamity" (3). As the narrative proceeds, however, it becomes apparent that Caleb aims at much more than a purely legal vindication.

To the word "innocence" are added other terms suggestive of broader qualities and often touching on key Godwinian concepts, terms such as "simplicity" and "sincerity." The insistence is not merely that Caleb is not a thief but also that he is innocent in more profound ways. He is, he implies, without guilt or sin. Exhibiting this purity in his youth and his early days at Falkland House, he has miraculously retained it through all the miseries and complexities of his relationship with Falkland. Thus, looking back on his career as a misunderstood man, he not only can prove his legal innocence but can relate his history with a Judgment Day honesty and rectitude, "the same simplicity and accuracy that I would observe towards a court which was to decide in the last resort upon every thing dear to me" (106).

In trying to seek out the precise nature of this vaunted innocence, the reader is likely to find himself in sympathy with Falkland, who at one point quotes with approval the dying words of Brutus: "O Virtue! I sought thee as a substance, but I find thee an empty name!" (117). For all the frequency with which Caleb invokes it, his innocence proves elusive and nebulous. Part of the reader's doubt arises from the very frequency with which Caleb resorts to the term to explain or justify his actions. Describing his first suspicion that Falkland is a murderer, and aware that "the reader will scarcely believe that the idea suggested itself to my mind," he immediately excuses himself on the grounds that: "It was but a passing thought; but it serves to mark the simplicity of my character" (107). The explanation is, in fact, open to objection on two counts. As the narrative makes clear, the suspicion is anything but passing. Moreover, the reader cannot lightly accept a definition of innocence or simplicity which includes such a readiness to believe evil of others; one imagines that innocence is distinguished by precisely the opposite tendency. When the suspicion has become translated into action, Caleb continues to use the idea of innocence in a similarly free and easy manner. During his inquisitorial interviews with Falkland, Caleb claims, his remarks are "artless and untaught," his effusions "innocent," while his behavior is distinguished by its "simple vivacity" (108–109).

These interviews with Falkland show not innocence but a convenient, false naiveté. Whether or not Caleb's actions are justifiable, it is clearly misleading to call them "innocent." Caleb himself admits as much when he refers to his own "air of innocence" and his "apparent want of design" (108). The effect of this admission, however, is somewhat decreased by his apparent lack of interest in drawing any distinction between the true and the false, between innocence and guile—a failing which he later insists to be one of the worst aspects of the world's opinion. Even after his duplicity has become apparent to Falkland, he can with casual confidence refer to the "sincerity of my manners" as "unvaried" (194).

Caleb's use of the idea of innocence serves to draw attention to both his unreliability as narrator and his dubious moral status. Obviously he is innocent—as he claims to be—in the strictly legal sense. The substance behind his other claims seems merely to be an initial naiveté, an "ignorance of the world" (8), which is distinguished primarily by the speed of its disappearance. This ignorance does not even qualify as that "cloistered virtue" of which Milton disapproved, for it is not a moral quality but simply a lack of practical experience. Caleb at the beginning of the book is the Lockean *tabula rasa:* a mind which has not yet received sufficient impressions to qualify as experienced.

Caleb's innocence is destroyed by his curiosity. He himself points to this quality as the mainspring of his character and the determinant of his fortunes. Listing its manifestations, he first mentions his "mechanical turn" (4), shown later in his mastery of such diverse skills as lockpicking, carpentry, acting, watchmaking, and writing. This vein of practical ingenuity, combined with a readiness to learn, aligns him with the tradition of sturdy Protestant heroes stemming from Robinson Crusoe. Coming from humble origins, Caleb sets out confidently as the master of his destiny. "The world," he tells Falkland in an attempt to convert him to the gospel of self-help, "was made for men of sense to do what they will with it" (117).

Fictional detectives are frequently characterized by pragmatism and by practical ingenuity. In Caleb's case, however, these qualities are strangely unrelated to that side of his curiosity which makes him turn detective. His resourcefulness and his willingness to learn are important primarily in helping him to resist and evade Falkland's tyranny, and are only marginally relevant to the events which provoke that tyranny. Caleb's ingenuity arises from a practical interest in the world around him and has an immediate, sometimes vital use. By contrast, his curiosity about Falkland is strictly nonutilitarian. Only after he has received final confirmation of his master's guilt does he think to ask himself: "What shall I do with the knowledge I have been so eager to acquire?" (130).

His eagerness is in response to an irrational obsession rather than a practical need. Caleb is the victim of "a kind of fatal impulse that seemed destined to hurry me to my destruction" (121). In imagery which suggests the similarity of his obsessive curiosity to Edgar Allan Poe's "imp of the perverse,"

Caleb speaks of the "demon" (119) which finally brings him to "the verge of the precipice" (138). That threatened abyss again takes a form familiar to readers of Poe: a paralysis of the will but not of the intellect: "To my own conception I was like a man, who, though blasted with lightning and deprived for ever of the power of motion, should yet retain the consciousness of his situation. Death-dealing despair was the only idea of which I was sensible" (134). This is the complete opposite of the condition to which his practical ingenuity brings him. Caleb's lockpicking activities in prison, for example, give him a measure of control over his own fate; but his curiosity about Falkland leads only to impotence and despair.

A similar habit of self-aggrandizement characterizes the way in which Caleb describes that side of his curiosity which prompts him to become a detective. He is, he explains near the beginning of the narrative, "a sort of natural philosopher" (4). Reflecting ruefully on the causes of his misfortunes, he remarks, "My offence had merely been a mistaken thirst of knowledge" (133). Such remarks are vague in reference but have the unmistakable effect of suggesting that the reader should view Caleb as a noble Faustian overreacher or a daring speculator. Godwin himself was dedicated to the principles of rational and revolutionary inquiry and showed in his later novel, *St. Leon,* an interest in the theme of the intellectual and moral overreacher. Such overtones, however, are misleading in the case of Caleb Williams.

In fact, Caleb's curiosity is of precisely the sort that he himself had previously designated as "ignoble" (4). He develops an interest in Falkland unadorned by either moral concern or intellectual originality. Rather, his master affords him "an ample field for speculation and conjecture" (6). As if to emphasize the point that Caleb's speculation is that of the gossip rather than the moral philosopher, the reader is told that the other servants in the house regard Falkland in a strikingly similar manner. Although, like Caleb, "they regarded him upon the whole with veneration as a being of superior order," "they would sometimes indulge their conjectures respecting his singularities" (7). Caleb in fact learns the vital information about Falkland's past from Mr. Collins in the form of an intriguing and morally edifying servants' anecdote. Although Caleb's curiosity eventually leads him into realms of moral and intellectual complexity which a Faust or a St. Leon might well inhabit, this is essentially an accident—one that he hardly welcomes—and not the result of any intention on his part. Rather than being the overreacher which his narrative tone at times suggests, Caleb the detective is more the Peeping Tom and the gossip, a figure who invites criticism.

Caleb enters Falkland's service a young and inexperienced man, ignorant of the ways of the world. Under the pressure of curiosity about his master's life he outgrows his initial naiveté, replacing it with a feigned naiveté, an "air of innocence." Godwin's firm disapproval of the type of social manner and behavior adopted by Caleb is on record elsewhere. "Insincerity," he writes in *The Enquirer*, "corrupts and empoisons the soul of the actor, and is of pernicious example to every spectator."[6] Indeed, sincerity—one of the terms that Caleb uses with so uncritical a liberality—is a vital concept in Godwin's vision of ideal social intercourse. However, the description of Caleb's activities as a detective does not reflect merely the social ethics of a philosopher who could on occasion take extreme positions. It also represents a specific response to contemporary issues.

In the novel Caleb is not called a "detective," for the term did not gain currency until the middle of the nineteenth century. He is called a "spy." The word first appears near the beginning of the narrative as part of Falkland's hysterical reaction to Caleb's accidental intrusion on him: "You set yourself as a spy upon my actions. But bitterly shall you repent your insolence. Do you think you shall watch my privacies with impunity?" (8). Later Caleb himself acknowledges the justice of the term first applied so contemptuously. After his decision to seek out the truth about Tyrrel's murder, he reflects gleefully on the prospect of being "a spy upon Mr. Falkland!" (107). Then, as now, the term could refer simply to "one who spies upon or watches a person or persons secretly."[7] In its more specialized sense it was applied to the professional snooper, in particular to the spy whose investigations served matters of foreign or military policy, or of internal security.

As the withdrawn Preface to the first edition indicates, Godwin aimed to write a novel of immediate relevance to contemporary political and social issues. In the 1790s internal political spying was just such an issue. During this period English radical agitation, catalyzed by the events in France, became the target of popular resentment and governmental repression. The process began with the activities of Church and King mobs, conservative vigilantes who attacked radicals' property and threatened their lives, and culminated in the passing of a series of emergency laws and in several political trials. From the start the radicals were convinced that the government was using spies against them. At times their suspicions verged on the hysterical: "If a Citizen made a Motion which seemed anyways spirited he was set down as a Spy sent among them by Government. If a Citizen sat in a Corner & said nothing he was watching their proceedings that he might the better report it . . . Citizens hardly knew how to act."[8]

Though sometimes ludicrous in their manifestations, the fears were well-founded. In its reaction to the threat posed by radical organizations, Pitt's government had set a precedent which later administrations were to follow during the Luddite and Chartist disturbances. At the trial for treason of Thomas Muir in August 1793, Anne Fisher—a spy and ex-servant in the Muir household—appeared as a prosecution witness. The following year no fewer than five spies gave evidence against Thomas Hardy and eleven other radicals accused of high treason.

When the involvement of Oliver the Spy with Jeremiah Brandreth and the Pentridge conspirators of 1817 came to light, there was widespread public concern about the governmental spy system. Together with Peterloo, the incident helped to make Castlereagh remembered with "a bitterness unique in the history of public men" for the "type of methods that are odious to the English nature." [9] No such furor, however, resulted from the appearance of spies at the 1790s trials, although their reception in court revealed public attitudes similar to those from which the later outcry grew.

At Hardy's trial the term "spy" was a dirty word. Both the prosecution and the defense were implicitly agreed that, though a spy's evidence might appear valuable, the fact that he was a spy could easily alienate the jury's sympathy. Accordingly, the prosecution avoided all reference to the profession of John Groves and his fellow spies who had collected the evidence against Hardy. Thomas Erskine, the skillful and flamboyant defense counsel, was continually concerned to force them to admit to the description "spy." He then flaunted it before them as incriminating evidence, at one point sneeringly addressing a witness as "good Mr. Spy."[10] Although the majority of people feared and disliked radicals, they regarded with equal distaste men whose profession involved eavesdropping on their fellows.

Godwin was deeply interested in these matters on both a personal and an ideological level. Several of the radicals on trial in 1794 were his "particular friends," and he wrote an eloquent pamphlet in defense of the accused men.[11] The trials themselves did not, of course, influence *Caleb Williams*, for they came after its composition. Rather, the novel grew out of the political milieu of which the trials are the clearest historical expression. Godwin chose to call Caleb a "spy" at a time when radicals were hyperconscious of the presence of political spies in their midst. Caleb is quite different in motivation from the men who gave evidence against Hardy: he has "no inclination to turn informer" (130) and does so only under the most extreme provocation. In effect, however, his investigation of Falkland is similar to the types of surveillance reported at the trials. He pries into his master's possessions and becomes increasingly adroit at insinuating conversations designed to force him into self-betrayal. The criticism of Caleb the detective and the hostility to the spy draw their life from the same ground.

The simplest example of this relationship is Caleb's fallibility and unreliability as a detective. At one point he says of Falkland's loss of control during their conversations: "These appearances I too frequently interpreted into grounds of suspicion, though I might with equal probability and more liberality have ascribed them to the cruel mortifications he had encountered in the objects of his darling ambition" (109). Attacking the idea of "a national militia of spies and informers" in *Considerations of Lord Grenville's and Mr. Pitt's Bills*, Godwin argues that this tendency to interpret all evidence in the light of preconceived suspicions is an occupational hazard of spying. The spy "undertakes to remember words, and he has an invincible bias upon his mind, inducing him to construe them in a particular way, and insensibly to change them for words more definite and injurious."[12]

Caleb and the political spy share deeper failings. Erskine provided an important clue to their source when at Hardy's trial he indulged in a mock panegyric on George Lynam, a spy who had joined a radical organization in order to report on its activities to the authorities: "O EXCELLENT EVIDENCE!—THE SUBSTANCE OF WORDS TAKEN DOWN BY A SPY, AND SUPPLIED, WHEN DEFECTIVE, BY HIS MEMORY. But I must not call him a spy; for it seems he took them *bonâ fide* as a delegate, and yet *bonâ fide* as an informer;—what a happy combination of fidelity! faithful to serve, and faithful to betray! correct to record for the business of the society, and correct to dissolve and punish it!"[13] The implication that such a "combination of fidelity" is far from happy lies at the heart of the issue. The spy was a suspect citizen because his profession involved precisely the opposite of those qualities of honor and honesty in which good citizenship has traditionally been rooted. Loyalty to the profession of spying involved disloyalty in the actual social relationships which form the basis of society. In its simplest form, as in the case of George Lynam, this conflict emerged as an incompatibility between the spy's loyalty to his employer and to the social group of which he was a sworn and trusted member. The defense of national security thus involved an assault upon social ethics.

Such fears were intensified when the spy was also a servant. In summing up for the defense at Hardy's trial, Erskine was able to adduce Edmund Burke in support of his attack upon spies. Burke had drawn attention to the alarming prospect of being spied on by "the very servant who waits behind your chair."[14] Burke's phrase was echoed by Godwin himself in one of his *Letters of Mucius*, where he reflects that the offering of rewards for the conviction of radicals would encourage "my very footman from behind my chair" to turn informer.[15] The fear had already been realized at the trial of Thomas Muir. In his speech in self-defense Muir singled out not the substance of Anne Fisher's evidence but the nature of her double profession as spy and servant for the target of his most purple rhetoric. Her behavior, he told the jury, "must rouse, as having domestics yourselves, your keenest indignation."[16]

In its disregard for conventionally upright conduct spying always contained an implicit threat to the social structure built on the traditional code of honor and loyalty. The threat took on added force in the context of the master-servant relationship, since—from the master's viewpoint—the relationship would have appeared as both a microcosm of the larger social order and a source of potential anxiety.

To the employer the servant was not merely a hired helper but also in some respects a part of the family unit. Falkland phrases his offer of employment to Caleb as the suggestion that he "take [him] into his family" (5), and Caleb later refers to himself and his fellow servants as part of "Mr. Falkland's family" (108). The term aptly describes the physical proximity of master and servant, who even reside in the same house. It also implies that the servant did not work merely for money but was also bound to his master by emotions and obligations similar to the familial. He owed his master not just service in the literal sense but also respect, deference, and loyalty. A relationship founded on mutual need was thus supplemented and stabilized by emotional bonds. To the master it would naturally appear as a reassuring symbol of social harmony and, indeed, of the social order itself.

At the same time the very appurtenances of order and harmony could easily be undermined. For all their closeness in certain respects, the master and servant remained essentially very different and distant. From his radical perspective Godwin was able to perceive in their relationship a striking epitome of what was later called the "two nations." The rich man's house, he observed in *The Enquirer*, "is inhabited by two classes of beings, or, more accurately speaking, by two sets of men drawn from two distant stages of barbarism and refinement."[17] The master of necessity and right maintained a certain aloofness from his domestics, but this often served to render them inscrutable, for their true personalities rarely emerged in his presence. Godwin himself, again in *The Enquirer*, remarked that a servant's job required him to exhibit "a studied countenance" to his employers.[18] As William Thackeray was later to discover, the reflection that the servant at one's elbow was virtually a complete stranger could become troubling. Only a slight disruption in the relationship could make the member of the family seem a serpent in the bosom.

Caleb Williams thus reflects not only the general hostility to spying but also the fear of the spy in its acutest form. That Caleb should be the servant of the man whose crime he uncovers is a fact of central importance to the narrative. Caleb's twin identity as servant and spy is implicit in his Christian name. His Biblical namesake was one of "the men which Moses sent to spy out the land" of Canaan.[19] Upon his return, Caleb was rewarded by Moses for fidelity of service: "But my servant Caleb, because he . . . hath followed me fully, him will I bring into the land whereinto he went; and his seed shall possess it."[20] The idea of fidelity is further enforced by the Hebrew derivation of the name from *Kalebh,* meaning "like a dog" and hence "faithful."

Godwin, with his Calvinist upbringing and his youthful experience as a minister, would certainly have been aware of these references. Indeed, throughout the book Caleb's roles as servant and spy are continually brought into juxtaposition. The occasion on which the term "spy" is first used of Caleb also draws attention to his social status. Falkland threatens him: "You set yourself as a spy upon my actions. But bitterly shall you repent your insolence. Do you think you shall watch my privacies with impunity?" (8). Later Falkland reproves Caleb's attempts to draw him into conversation as "improper" (119) and warns him, "learn to be more respectful!" (118). In each case the criticism invokes not an abstract moral code but a code of conduct dictated by their positions as master and servant.

The implicit comparison between Caleb's spying and his job as servant is continued in the sentence which announces his decision to embark upon detection: "I determined to place myself as a watch upon my patron" (107). More commonly Caleb refers to Falkland simply as "Mr. Falkland," a denomination that in the passage preceding this quotation he uses twice. The reader's attention is thus caught by the shift at a crucial moment to the term of sociological reference, "my patron."[21] Caleb's use of the word "employment" also juxtaposes his roles as servant and spy. Initially the word is used to refer to his job as Falkland's secretary-cum-servant: "if . . . I approved of the employment" (5); "My employment was easy and agreeable" (6). Later Caleb applies the term to his activities as detective: "The instant I had chosen this employment for myself, I found a strange sort of pleasure in it . . . That there was danger in the employment served to give an alluring pungency to the choice" (107).

This deliberate juxtaposition is ironic. It enforces the same basic point made by Erskine in his comments on George Lynam's actions. Caleb, like Lynam, cannot have things both ways. A combination of faithful service and efficient surveillance is impossible, for spying requires of Caleb a violation of the duties involved in his assigned social role. The breach of fidelity takes on particular significance within the context of the master-servant relationship.

From the beginning of the narrative it is made clear that Falkland, despite the eccentricities caused by his private guilt, is in the salient respects a model employer. Such a role would come naturally to a character who draws his inspiration from the ideal of benevolence best exemplified by Samuel Richardson's portrait of Sir Charles Grandison. "His manner was kind, attentive and humane" (5), Caleb reports of their first meeting, adding: "My reception was as gracious and encouraging as I could possibly desire. Mr. Falkland questioned me respecting my learning, and my conceptions of men and things, and listened to my answers with condescension and approbation. This kindness soon restored to me a considerable part of my self-possession, though I still felt restrained by the graceful, but unaltered dignity of his carriage" (5). On the one hand, Falkland's behavior implicitly asserts the master's right to keep his servants at a respectful distance. On the other, his manner shows a kindness and sensitivity appropriate to the local squire who is offering to bring an orphaned youth under the protection of his "family." In view of this latter characteristic, Caleb's suspicions have about them an air of churlish ingratitude. They represent, as it were, a refusal to return kind attentions with kind thoughts. However, the burden of the criticism falls not so much on the suspicions themselves as on the course of conduct that they lead Caleb to pursue.

The air of frankness that he feigns in his conversations with

Falkland in fact represents an exaggerated version of that "studied countenance" which Godwin noted in all servants. Inscrutability becomes supplemented by a calculated deceptiveness. From Falkland's point of view the effect is to increase the gap that separates him from his servant. From Caleb's viewpoint the gap is narrowed, for he renders himself deliberately unknowable in order to penetrate his master's privacies more successfully. On the psychological level, Caleb attempts to delve into the hidden recesses of his master's mind, to uncover the source of his private anguish. On the physical level, his activities involve a violation of his master's private possessions. He reads the letter from Hawkins, the man hanged for Tyrrel's murder, and attempts to examine the contents of Falkland's trunk at a point when his duties as servant clearly require him to help prevent his master's house burning down.[22]

As Falkland had earlier protested of Caleb's accidental intrusion on him, such actions are a type of "insolence" (8), of social presumption and disrespect. Refusing to view his master's affairs from a respectful distance, Caleb is claiming an intimacy with Falkland to which even a social equal would have no right. By thus converting himself into Falkland's inquisitor rather than his servant, Caleb is not merely offending against the initial terms of the relationship, but threatening to reverse them. Burke foresaw that the end result of the spy-servant's activities would be to render the gentleman's social inferior "the arbiter of [his] life and fortune."[23] Despite Falkland's repeated and eventually tyrannical assertions of squirearchical power, Caleb is able to make Burke's fear come true. In the book's climactic scene he, like Anne Fisher, becomes a successful informer on the man to whom, according to the social code, he owes respect and loyalty.

Thus, although Caleb begins his detection with the interests of a gossip, he develops into a mischief-maker of a peculiarly potent sort. The magistrate's expostulation when Caleb finally presents evidence against Falkland reflects a very real fear in the contemporary audience: "There would be a speedy end to all order and good government, if fellows that trample upon ranks and distinctions in this atrocious sort, were upon any consideration suffered to get off" (276). The criticism is one that Caleb himself cannot entirely discount. Though it only serves to add spice to the adventure, he is on occasion uneasily aware of the "forbidden" (107) nature of his investigations. At one point, he defines the nature of this forbidden territory in a phrase that significantly foreshadows the magistrate's accusation. He has, he confesses, been "trampling on the established boundaries of obligation" (138).

To this analysis of the judgments passed on Caleb it may be objected that they suggest a surprising degree of accord between Godwin the radical philosopher and the middle-class public of his day, as they imply an agreement between Godwin and Falkland, the epitome of the established system. The answer to the objection is that, on the issue of spying, such agreement exists. Caleb's detection involves a disregard for those basic qualities—sincerity and sensitivity—upon which Godwin's ideal social code was based. Also, in the 1790s a radical would have had special reasons for being hostile toward the spy. *Caleb Williams* was after all written by a man who had envisaged the possibility of being prosecuted for his previous book.[24] In the last analysis, however, the condemnation of Caleb's conduct as servant-spy depends on the particular nature of Godwin's own radicalism.

Godwin himself attacked the institution of service as an example of "the madness of artificial society."[25] However, this did not lead him to sympathize with Caleb's resolute flouting of the conduct appropriate to servants. Though Falkland's later treatment of Caleb is identified with that social tyranny which Godwin so hated, Caleb's actions also strongly resemble that rash revolutionism which the author criticized in his fellow radicals. Godwin's political writings look forward to the gradual evolution of a Utopian society while ruling out the desirability of revolution in the streets.

Eschewing revolution as a means of attaining his ideal goals, Godwin often adopts a stance of modified liberalism. It is perhaps unfortunate that his thought should be best known through *Political Justice*, a work which avowedly concentrates on abstract theory and favors expressions of absolute disapproval of various social institutions. As *The Enquirer* and the pamphlet writings show, Godwin had a flexible mind, and his practical response was usually to accept the fact that such institutions were here to stay for at least the foreseeable future and to suggest ways in which they might be made more liberal and humane.

To *Caleb Williams* this habit leads to a distribution of sympathy between Caleb, the assailant of the social order, and Falkland, the representative of "things as they are." Though Godwin later agrees with Caleb's fulminations against the system, he also sympathizes with Falkland's protests against the implications of Caleb's conduct as a spy. Falkland's angry dismissal of the detective as an "insolent domestic" (118) thus carries with it the endorsement of a writer who in practice often showed a cautious and pragmatic acquiescence to current institutions.

In *Caleb Williams* detection is not merely a transgression of social etiquette; it is also a complex psychological process that further renders Caleb's status as hero dubious. He achieves the intimacy with Falkland that he so passionately desires, but it proves a curse rather than a blessing. As his investigations progress, Caleb plunges deeper and deeper into moral uncertainties. Caleb and Falkland begin to resemble each other, and their fates become inextricably linked; by the end of the novel, detective and criminal appear more like symbiotic twins than antagonists.

Although Caleb's ultimate conduct toward his master smacks of churlish ingratitude, his initial response is a profound—indeed, an exaggerated—respect. In a book replete with purple rhetoric his declarations of feeling for Falkland loom especially hyperbolic. Falkland, as the "patron" of a recently orphaned youth, discharges responsibilities similar to the paternal, and Caleb's reactions indicate an eager acceptance of the role of surrogate son. "From the first moment I saw him, I conceived the most ardent admiration" (321). Indeed, Caleb's "ardent admiration" surpasses the bounds of filial warmth and becomes a type of religious devotion.

Speaking in the book's climactic scene of his earlier attitude, Caleb declares: "I have reverenced him; he was worthy of reverence: I have loved him; he was endowed with qualities that partook of divine" (320–321). Initially experiencing a sense of "awe" (5) in Falkland's presence, Caleb later graduates to "the most complete veneration" (122). When he hears his master's history from Mr. Collins, Caleb converts Falkland into a Christ-like figure with virtues "almost too sublime for human nature," the victim of "sufferings so unexampled, so unmerited" (107), "more an angel than a man" (119). In the latter part of the book Caleb, in implicit acknowledgment of his sense of guilt, describes his ex-master's persecution as the vengeance of the stern Calvinist God: "It was like what has been described of the eye of omniscience pursuing the guilty sinner, and darting a ray that awakens him to new sensibility, at the very moment that, otherwise, exhausted nature would lull him into a temporary oblivion of the reproaches of his conscience" (305).

Seen in this context, Caleb's assumption of the role of detective appears an act of involuntary iconoclasm against the idol he himself has created, a surrender to "the demon that possessed me" (119). Significantly, one of his first actions as a detective is to launch an oblique attack on Falkland by voicing doubts about the character of Alexander the Great, who attempted to "persuade mankind that he was the son of Jupiter Ammon" (111). Caleb cites the opinions of Fielding and Doctor Prideaux, which Falkland considers to be "Accursed blasphemy!" (110). But blasphemy is always an ambiguous activity, and disbelief does not supplant veneration in Caleb's mind. In fact, the story that originally sows the seed of suspicion also provides him with "a thousand fresh reasons to admire and love Mr. Falkland" (106). Caleb becomes the victim of "a contention of opposite principles that by turns usurped dominion over my conduct" (122). Veneration continues in uneasy juxtaposition to his newly awakened suspicions, and his characteristic sensation during his investigations is mental "uncertainty and restlessness" (122).

Caleb's discovery of the truth about Falkland's past merely intensifies his emotional turbulence. He had earlier promised himself "an unknown gratification" (122) in the achievement of the secret, and he celebrated its pursuit as a means toward maturity and the expansion of his powers. It proves, however, to be an initiation into a world of frightening experience: "The ease and light-heartedness of my youth were for ever gone. The voice of an irresistible necessity had commanded me to 'sleep no more' " (138).

In his "mistaken thirst of knowledge" (133) Caleb has encountered the problem of evil in a peculiarly complex and disturbing form. During his investigations he had been uneasily aware of their forbidden nature, if only in the most obvious sense that they went against Falkland's commands. He discovered that, despite his good intentions and his earnestness, he contained the seeds of evil within himself; he could, as he confesses to Falkland, yield to a "demon" (119). This truth—that good and evil can exist in a single character in close juxtaposition—is again demonstrated by the revelation of Falkland's crime. Earlier Caleb had oscillated between the belief that his master was the "best of men" (120) and the suspicion that he was a murderer. By hearing Falkland's confession, he is brought to the realization that his master is in fact both. Caleb does not learn that Falkland is a bad man, nor that he is a good man gone bad; rather, he learns that Falkland is simultaneously both good and bad. "Mr. Falkland is a murderer! resumed I. He might yet be a most excellent man, if he did but think so" (137).

Expressed in abstract terms, the truth that Caleb has discovered is that good and evil, though apparently worlds apart, are in practice bedfellows. In his relationship with Falkland, Caleb enacts this truth for the rest of the novel. Rather than appearing as simple polar opposites, the detective and the criminal become inextricably connected. As Caleb remarks by way of preface to the narrative of Falkland's past, "To his story the whole fortune of my life was linked" (10). Their destinies are finally interdependent. The tragedy of Caleb hinges on the tragedy of Falkland, and the tragedy of Falkland hinges on the tragedy of Caleb.

This close structural relationship is emphasized by the emotional bonds that develop between the detective and the criminal. Caleb eventually achieves an intimacy with Falkland, though of a type he neither expected nor welcomes. He has sympathy for Falkland: "I felt, what I had no previous conception of, that it was possible to love a murderer, and, as I then understood it, the worst of murderers" (130). The deceptions necessary to his investigation instill in him a sense of guilt which gives him "a fellow feeling for other offenders" (138). As the investigation proceeds, a "magnetical sympathy" (112) develops between them. Describing Falkland adjudicating the case of the peasant accused of murder, Caleb records: "The ex-amination had not proceeded far before he chanced to turn his eye to the part of the room where I was. It happened in this, as in some preceding instances; we exchanged a silent look by which we told volumes to each other" (126).

After the discovery of Falkland's secret this extrasensory contact develops into a mental haunting. When apart, each is unable to rid himself of the mental presence of the other. After Caleb's departure from the manor and escape from prison, Falkland persists in remaining obsessed by his very existence. Even after his ex-master's death Caleb cannot forget him: "His figure is ever in imagination before me. Waking or sleeping I still behold him" (325). Brought together by their obsessive natures, they conclude by becoming obsessed with each other. The process involves something approaching a destruction of their separate identities. They become almost fragmented halves of a single personality. When Caleb announces that "My heart bleeds at the recollection of his misfortunes as if they were my own" (10), the figure of speech is no idle one.

This destruction of their separate identities is aided by the manner in which Caleb progressively comes to resemble Falk-land. The effect of detection upon Caleb is like the effect of the crime itself upon Falkland. The servant develops the master's desperate "sensibility to reputation" (101); this is actually his main motive for writing his memoirs. Energetic and youthful, he had initially appeared the antithesis of his decaying and neurotic master. Having become the sole sharer of Falkland's secret, unable to blot out the knowledge and reluctant to com-municate it to others, Caleb ages as Falkland himself had aged after Tyrrel's death. He loses "the ease and light-heartedness" (138) of youth. As in the case of Falkland, the loss of youth as a psychological condition is reflected in the loss of physical youth. Falkland's obvious decay is discreetly paralleled by a debilitation on Caleb's part. As the narrative nears its end, Caleb grows closer and closer to Falkland's state of physical and emotional weakness. Shortly before confronting the semi-paralyzed Falkland, Caleb reports: "My fits of despondence were deeper and of more frequent occurrence. My health every day grew worse" (268).

Their final confrontation, when Caleb at last publicly accuses his master of murder, brings to a climax the emotional bond and the similarity between the two men. The intimacy which Caleb's earlier detection had initiated is symbolically culminated and acknowledged. Caleb reports that in a final gesture Falkland "rose from his seat supported by the attendants, and—to my infinite astonishment—threw himself into my arms" (324). The master resigns himself to the fact that his name will be "consecrated to infamy" (324), while the servant concludes: "I began these memoirs with the idea of vindicating my character. I have now no character that I wish to vindicate" (326). What Falkland had earlier confessed to him, Caleb is now able to confess to the court: "In thus acting I have been a murderer" (323).

During one of his insinuating conversations with his master, Caleb had remarked that "innocence and guilt are too much confounded in human life" (117). He was referring to the fallibility of the world's opinion, but his remark might apply in another sense to the world to which his detective activities have introduced him. For the final effect of the relationship between the detective and the criminal is to introduce ambiguities on the psychological level similar to those on the social level. Detection begins as an activity apparently designed to establish moral and intellectual clarity. The detective, voluntarily or involuntarily, assumes the role of an agent of justice, seeking to distinguish good from evil and to identify the source of evil. Caleb's relationship with Falkland, however, progressively suggests that good and evil do not admit of so simple a polarization. Inextricably linked, the detective and the criminal are similar in their characters and in their fates. Rather than emerging as antithetical or antagonistic in their relations, they grow into symbiotic twins. In this respect, Godwin is opening up a mine for later writers. In "The Purloined Letter" Poe's Monsieur Dupin encounters an opponent who seems in many respects the mirror image of himself. And the climax of *Caleb Williams*, when the dying Falkland throws himself into his accuser's arms, is echoed a century later in the deadly embrace of Holmes and Moriarty at the Reichenbach Falls.

3
Vidocq Translated

Caleb Williams demonstrated for the first time that the detective could become the focus of serious literary interest. During the first half of the nineteenth century this process was continued, though in widely differing ways, in the work of Balzac and Poe. But in England between the publication of Godwin's novel in the closing years of the eighteenth century and the contribution of Dickens, which belongs to the middle years of the nineteenth, no writer of importance turned with sustained attention to the subject of the detective.

Yet in the society as a whole there was no lack of interest, and the period saw important changes affecting the detective's role. The Bow Street Runners, that small and rudimentary detective corps originating in the reforms of Henry and John Fielding, achieved a prominent reputation. In 1829 the Metropolitan Police was established under Peel's guidance, supplemented in 1842 by a special department devoted to detective work, the successor to the Runners and the ancestor of the modern Criminal Investigation Department. Since police and detectives had long been topics of controversy, these changes were accompanied by widespread debate as well as by a gradual shift in public attitude.

Such important historical developments are commonly reflected, with whatever crudities and distortions, in popular literature. From the late 1820s onward several works, popular in their own time though now all but forgotten, dealt with police detectives, providing primitive footnotes to social history. They form a minor counterpart to the mass of contemporary literature dealing with the criminal. Their customary form was borrowed from the perennially popular "true confessions" of convicted criminals. Laying claims to authenticity, these works posed as "memoirs" or "reminiscences" of real-life detectives, being in fact either grossly fictionalized or wholly fictive.

Two important and related patterns are apparent in this literature. The detective emerges as a defined literary stereotype: conventions of characterization are established, recur, and eventually become inflexible and ritualized. This development is accompanied by a change in the detective's status. Beginning as a suspect though often entertaining rogue, he finally becomes a hero of a less ambiguous sort: a solidly middle-class citizen whose values reflect those of the writer and his audience. An important transition is thus effected. The detective moves from the world of the eighteenth century, of Jonathan Wild and Caleb Williams, to the world of Dickens' Inspector Bucket.

The most influential contribution to this process came from France, in the work of Eugène-François Vidocq, head of the Surêté, the main detective force. Born at Arras in 1775, Vidocq enjoyed a career both more adventurous and less respectable than his official status might suggest. In his youth he ran away from home, joined the army, and deserted. Imprisoned, he found himself accused and convicted of forging a document used in the escape of some fellow-prisoners, a crime which he consistently denied. Thereafter his career as a convict was marked by numerous and often successful attempts at escape—from Bicêtre and La Force, as well as from the galleys of Toulon and Brest. After achieving notoriety as a latter-day Jack Sheppard, he approached the Paris police with the offer of his services as an informer and detective.

In France the reliance upon the motto "Set a thief to catch a thief" was even greater than in England, and the prisons provided a continual source of recruits for the police force. After some delay Vidocq's proposal was accepted. First, he worked as an informer while remaining in prison, and then, granted his liberty, he posed as a fugitive galley-slave amidst the Paris underworld. In 1812 he was appointed chief of the newly formed Surêté, a post he held until 1827. After retirement Vidocq's life was no less colorful. He managed a paper factory staffed largely by ex-convicts, briefly returned to his old job at the Surêté, published several books, ran a private detective agency, participated in political intrigues, and visited London with an exhibition composed of paintings, artificial fruit, criminal curios, and himself. He finally died in poverty in 1857.

In England the main vehicle of Vidocq's considerable fame was his *Memoirs*, published in Paris in 1828–1829 and quickly translated. For readers of an age when the reminiscences of public officials are not noted for liveliness, much less raciness, the work comes as a pleasant surprise. It is a good-humored, fast-moving, heterogeneous compilation of anecdotes and incidents, ranging in form from the jokebook to the social tract. The main narrative thread is provided by the successive metamorphoses of the hero: from adventurous and amorous youth, to army deserter, to convict and galley slave, to prison-breaker and habitué of the underworld, and finally to detective. But this thread is often tenuous. Particularly in the final volume, the account of Vidocq's life is continually interrupted by a wide variety of interpolations: the story of Capdeville, the burglar who charms his way into the confidence of susceptible widows; the sentimental tale of Adèle, reduced to crime and finally to suicide by poverty and neglect; urgent and often cogent attacks on the system of criminal justice and the current prejudice against ex-convicts; attempts to categorize criminals into classes, and to instruct the public in outwitting them.

The Introduction to the English edition promises readers a narrative "teeming with the wild and wonderful" (I,vi), and a gratified writer in the *Westminster Review* found the *Memoirs* "as amusing as a romance."[1] In fact, they are a romance. In his Preface Vidocq himself complains bitterly of alterations made in the facts by his editor, "one of those pretended men of letters, whose excessive impudence conceals their stupidity, and who had no other object in view than to make money" (I,xiii). The editing, he alleges, has blackened his character, and his enemies have contrived "to garble my Memoirs in such a way as to paralyze beforehand the effect of those discoveries on which they would have little cause for self-gratulation" (I,xvi).

It would be unwise to take these accusations at face value. From what is known of Vidocq's character, it would be entirely consistent if they were merely an attempt to gain extra publicity for the book. Nevertheless, it is certain the *Memoirs* are not Vidocq's own work: the names of Emile Morice and Louis-François L'Héritier are usually cited as the ghost writers.[2] The presence of a foreign hand is everywhere apparent. Profuse classical allusions do not, or at least so one imagines, flow readily from the pens of ex-convicts and ex-detectives. The book, moreover, is replete with minor acts of plagiarism. The English translator pointed out a debt to Patrick Colquhoun's *Police of the Metropolis*, where the French

writer had distorted an English place name with all the cheer-
ful aplomb of the fictive author of Swinburne's *La Fille du Policeman*. The tale of Adèle, which occupies an inordinate por-
tion of the fourth volume, had already been published as a
novel under L'Héritier's own name.[3]

The total effect is not merely to make the memoirs unreliable
as history; they are unredeemably fictional in form and spirit.
As Régis Messac has advised in his discussion of Vidocq, the
Memoirs should be read as a work of imagination.[4] Whether as
the result of the ghost writers' inventiveness or of the detective's own propensity for tall-story-telling, Vidocq's life is re-
cast according to the literary conventions of the day. His career
becomes a picaresque novel whose hero owes as much to Gil
Blas as to life. Of doubtful value as a social document, the
memoirs thus enjoy a position of peculiar literary importance.
They show the bare historical bones of the detective's character being remodeled into a commercially marketable form and
transformed into fictional convention.

Conceived as the stuff of legend and designed to attract the
interest of readers of popular literature, the portrait of Vidocq
establishes the detective as a striking and sharply defined
character. For all its careful exploration of the psychology and
ethics of detection, *Caleb Williams* had remained a strangely
disembodied study. The hero was eventually a reflective narrative voice rather than a completely individualized or sharply
realized actor in the plot. The book, its tone implied, was a
confession of the spirit rather than a drama of the flesh. Although Vidocq's *Memoirs* shares the form of autobiographical
narrative, it locates the detective in a world of physical reality
and vigorous action and portrays him in bold two-color terms.

Central to his characterization is the myth of infallibility,
carefully established and fully illustrated in the course of the
narrative. Vidocq the detective is an all-powerful and omniscient figure. The *Memoirs* is essentially an exercise in self-
aggrandizement, and Vidocq's own boasts continually draw
the reader's attention to his superhuman powers and achieve-
ments: "Never had any period been marked with more important discoveries than that which ushered in my début in the
service of the police; although scarcely enrolled in this administration, I had already done much for the safety of the

capital, and even for the whole of France. Were I to relate half my successes in my new department, my reader's patience would be exhausted" (II,158). Speaking of his apprenticeship as a detective, he remarks: "Not a day passed in which I did not effect some important discovery. Nothing escaped me, either relating to crimes which had been committed, or were in contemplation. I was in all places; I knew all that was passing or projecting; and never were the police idly or unprofitably employed when set to work upon my suggestions" (II,189). Elsewhere he claims to have been responsible for the capture of four thousand criminals in less than seven years—an average of nearly two a day.

The boasting is not confined to narrative commentary. As actor in the drama, Vidocq is equally concerned to impress the legend of the Great Detective on his colleagues, his clients, and his victims. Brought in to handle a case in which a jeweler has been robbed, he is asked by his superior:

"Well, Vidocq, what think you of it?"
"The affair is difficult," I answered to M. Henry, "but I will undertake it, and shall not be surprised if I come out of it with honour."
"Ah!" said M. Senard, squeezing my hand affectionately, "you restore me to life; spare nothing, I beseech you, Monsieur Vidocq; go to any expense requisite to arrive at a fortunate result. My purse is open to you, whatever be the sacrifice. Well, do you think you will succeed?"
"Yes, Sir, I do." (III,148)

Such scenes impart to the *Memoirs* an air of solemnly fantastic myth and give rise to a humor which the author does not intend; but the myth-making is not without a practical purpose. The detective is a zealous self-publicist, seeking to make his name sound "more harshly in the ears of the cabal [the underworld], than did that of the Just on the ears of the ancient Athenians, as as applied to Aristides" (III,47). Nothing succeeds, Vidocq believes, like the reputation for success. He aims to strike terror into the heart of the underworld by appearing a modern Nemesis, implacable and infallible.

This audacious and canny grasp of public relations is typical of his approach to the business of detection. Existing in an intensely physical milieu of exciting action and crude drama, Vidocq has little of the ratiocinator about him. Rather than bringing to his work new or specialized skills, he relies on familiar and traditional qualities raised to the pitch of greatness. He is, as the Introduction to the English edition proclaims, a man of "acuteness, activity, and courage" (I,ix). In his detective adventures he combines the bravery and the physical energy of the adventurer with the sharp-wittedness of the traditional picaresque hero.

His methods are well illustrated by the case of Moiselet. A parish priest and his friend, "one of the richest jewellers of the Palais Royal" (III,144), agree on the need to conceal their valuables from a troop of soldiers whose arrival in their village is expected shortly. They decide that it would be best to have the treasure buried and select Moiselet, sexton of the church and "the very pearl of honest fellows" (III,145), to do the job. After the soldiers have left, Moiselet comes to the clergyman with news that the buried valuables have disappeared. The police are consulted, and Vidocq is assigned to the case.

From the start his suspicions fall on the apparently trustworthy Moiselet, who is questioned and detained. But all Vidocq's attempts to gain proof of the sexton's guilt or a clue to the treasure's whereabouts fail. Finally, he disguises himself as a German servant and begins "to ramble about the vicinity . . . with a design of being apprehended" (III,150–151). Taken up as a suspicious vagabond, he is put in the same prison where Moiselet is detained. Meeting the suspect for the first time, he discerns a "refinement of roguery" (III,152) beneath the man's air of honesty and respectability:

[He] called me *Landsman* in that soft silky tone, which is always acquired by those church rats who are wont to live on the meats of the altar. He was not over fat; but that was constitutional with him, and, his leanness apart, he was glowing with health: he had a narrow forehead, small brown eyes sunk in his head, an enormous mouth, and although, in detailing his characteristics, some of a very sinister kind might be seen, the whole had that gentle air which would tempt the Devil to open the gates of Paradise; besides, to complete the portrait, this personage was at least four of five generations behindhand in costume, a circumstance which, in a country where the Gerontes can

make reputation for honesty, always establishes a presumption in favour of the individual. (III,151–152)

Liberally applying alcohol and flattery, the disguised Vidocq
works his way into his victim's confidence. Presenting himself
as a shiftless and dishonest character, he anticipates reciprocal
confessions from Moiselet. The ploy is unsuccessful, but Vidocq perseveres. He proposes that they escape from prison
together and flee to Germany. Moiselet agrees, and with the
discreet help of the prison authorities, the escape is effected.
As they are on the point of leaving the area, Moiselet stops to
retrieve the stolen treasure from the place where he has hidden it. Vidocq promptly sheds his disguise and arrests the as-
tonished thief:

> "No resistance," I said, "or I will cleave your skull in
> two."
> At this threat he seemed in a dream; but when he knew
> that he was gripped by that iron hand which has subdued
> the most vigorous malefactors, he was convinced that it
> was no vision. Moiselet was as quiet as a lamb. I had
> sworn not to leave him, and kept my word. During the
> journey to the station of the brigade of gendarmerie,
> where I deposited him, he frequently cried out,
> "I am done—who could have thought it? and he had
> such a simple look too!" (III,157)

Vidocq's methods here are typical, repeated in one form or
another in the numerous detective anecdotes which form the
substance of the later volumes of the *Memoirs*. To his job he
brings a formidably encyclopedic knowledge of the underworld, acquired during his disreputable youth: a thorough
grasp of the methods of criminals and the workings of prison
life. His ability to identify criminals and to predict their ruses
is aided by an intuitive skill in divining people's true characters. At one point he is able to discern the traitorous intentions of a police colleague merely by "fixing on him one of
those looks which penetrate the very heart's core" (II,225). His
energy and patience are limitless. Assigned to watch a house
during a freezing winter night, he half buries himself in a fer-
menting dunghill rather than desert his post. "At five in the
morning, I was still in my lurking-place, where I did very

well, except from the fumes which invaded my nostrils"
(II,208). In one adventure he combs the streets of Paris armed
with only the vaguest of clues: the criminal he seeks lives in
an apartment with yellow curtains, in the same building as a
hump-backed seamstress. At the end of another equally ardu-
ous hunt he remarks with uncharacteristic understatement,
"lack of perseverance is not my fault" (III,176).

Above all, disguise is the hallmark of his procedure. Claiming to possess "the strange faculty . . . of reducing my height
four or five inches, at pleasure" (II,143) and taking delight in
his skill as a make-up artist, the Vidocq of the *Memoirs* is an
exhaustively Protean personality, the man of a thousand
masks. Usually posing as a friend or accomplice of his victims,
he throws himself into his role with enthusiasm and a sense of
irony. In one episode he agrees to take part in a plan to assas-
sinate Vidocq; in another he acts out for the entertainment of
his criminal associates a little charade of Vidocq's downfall.
His evidence complete, he springs his trap with a melodramatic flourish. Having won the confidence of Pons Gérard, a
notorious murderer, he deliberately leads the conversation
round to the subject of Vidocq, the famous detective:

> "Well, I would advise him to keep out of my reach," ex-
> claimed Pons. "If he were here, I'll engage he would pass
> the worst quarter of an hour he ever experienced in his
> life."
> "Oh! you are like all the rest of them, talking of what
> you would do; and yet if he were before you at this mo-
> ment, you would sit perfectly still, and be the first to offer
> him a glass of wine." (At the time I was saying this I held
> out my glass, which he filled.)
> "I! I offer him wine! May a thousand devils seize me
> first!"
> "Yes, you, I say, would invite him to drink with you."
> "I tell you I would die sooner."
> "Then you may die as soon as your please, for *I* am
> Vidocq, and I arrest you!" (III,239)

Vidocq proved an influential character, the prototype of Balzac's Vautrin and Gaboriau's Monsieur Lecoq and an indirect
inspiration behind Poe's Monsieur Dupin. More generally, the
Memoirs introduced a number of motifs with which the fic-

tional detective was to be associated throughout the century, in both England and France. With his omnipotence and infallibility, his vast knowledge of criminal life, his energy, and particularly his fondness for disguise, Vidocq was the progenitor of countless detectives of fictive memoirs, novels, and melodramas. Refined and developed by succeeding writers, the portrayal eventually became one of the favorite stereotypes of popular literature.

Yet the *Memoirs*, standing at the beginning of a tradition which was eventually to glorify and adulate the detective, were written at a time when detectives in France and England were commonly the objects of suspicion and hostility. The French police, though known for their efficiency, also enjoyed an unenviable but apparently justified reputation for being corrupt and for acting as political spies. Embarking on his new career, Vidocq himself meditates on "the general odium attached to the department I filled" (II,187). His narrative, in fact, is an exercise in self-exoneration as well as self-aggrandizement: it is Vidocq's answer to his enemies and detractors.

His early life is presented as a continual battle against misunderstanding and injustice. He is, he insists, guiltless of the forgery for which he is convicted. An innocent man, he finds himself trapped in the sordid life of the prisons and galleys, surrounded by the most depraved of criminals. Despite the pressures of the environment, he manages to remain uncorrupted: "it never entered into my calculations to enrol myself in a band of thieves; for although I had associated with robbers, and lived by my wits, I felt an invincible repugnance to entering on a career of crimes, of which early experience had taught me the perils and risks" (I,163–164). Once in prison, he tries to escape, and once out of prison, he tries to lead an honest life. In these attempts, however, he is continually the victim of a "fatality which I was compelled to submit to unresistingly" (II,83). The police dog his tracks, and his prison associates seek him out to tempt him into joining their plans or, on one occasion, to blackmail him into financing their exploits.

Vidocq becomes a detective for much the same reason that he had been so incorrigible a prison-breaker: he wishes to escape his former life and be accepted into normal society. His enrollment in the police, as the Introduction explains to English readers, "did not result from a fear of danger or a spirit of treachery; the urgent motives that led VIDOCQ to this measure, were the desire of avoiding the perpetual contact with the vile scum with whom his lot was cast, and the knowledge that he could benefit his country, and thus pay recompense for past misconduct. Above all he could then enjoy liberty, and have before him the encouraging prospect of a reinstatement in society" (I,ix).

Being a detective is better than being a convict, but it hardly guarantees the respectability that Vidocq claims to seek. His aim in the later part of the narrative is to defend his own conduct as a policeman and to exalt the social value of his chosen profession. He declares his innocence of the accusations commonly leveled against French detectives: he does not undertake political surveillance, and he disapproves of the tactics of the *agent provocateur*. His denunciation of provocation receives special emphasis, being reprinted on the title page of the first volume in both the English and French editions. Though he gleefully exposes the corruptions of his police colleagues, his own honesty and incorruptibility are stressed. He presents himself to the reader, in highly melodramatic terms, as a servant of the public and a champion of the social order against its enemies: "the Hercules for whom was reserved the purging the earth of dire monsters, and cleansing out the Augean stable" (II,259).

Even though the reader accepts that Vidocq, unlike most of his colleagues, observes a minimal honesty, the self-portrait is not entirely persuasive. Vidocq's commentary on his life remains strangely at odds with much about that life which the narrative itself reveals. The idea of a respectable Vidocq remains unrealized, just as the portrait of Vidocq the innocent victim of circumstances fails to convince. He is too much the controversialist, too energetic and too flamboyant, to fit into a simple pattern of self-help and moral regeneration. In the early part of his memoirs, though technically innocent of the charges on which he is imprisoned, he is clearly a trickster and adventurer at heart. Inhabiting a literary form which takes its cue from the picaresque, he conforms to the pattern of the rogue hero: sexually amoral, geographically mobile, outwitting both prison authorities and police with zestful canniness.

Nor does his entry into the police force signify any deep change of character. Vidocq the detective merely uses the methods of Vidocq the convict—skill in disguise and a knowledge of the underworld—for rather than against the law. Moreover, his work for the police exhibits the same amorality which had earlier guided his life as adventurer. The essence of his technique is deception and betrayal, and in a moment of self-revelation he concedes that the patron saint of his profession is "Monsieur Judas" (III,97). He proclaims a ruthless belief that, in fighting the criminal, the end justifies the means. After describing how he tricked a woman into revealing her husband's guilt, he comments:

> Some persons may perhaps blame the expedient to which I had recourse, in order to free Paris from a receiver of stolen property, who had been for a long time a positive nuisance to the capital. Whether it be approved or not, I have at least the consciousness of having done my duty; besides when we wish to overreach scoundrels who are at open war with society, every stratagem is allowable by which to effect their conviction, except endeavouring to provoke the commission of crime. (II,193)

Despite such protestations, a love of the public welfare seems a less important motive in him than does a love of stratagem itself. Vidocq's world is one where the supreme values are naked intelligence and self-interest rather than justice or morality. "Don't you know," he chides one of his victims, "that the most crafty man is he who prospers best in this world?" (III,136).

This amorality makes Vidocq a disturbing as well as an entertaining figure. The omniscience and omnipotence to which he vociferously lays claim have a double effect. While they make him seem a superhuman hero, they also make him appear an inhuman monster. Legends about his employment by the police force abound, he tells the reader. It is said, for example, that to "obtain his liberty he has engaged to deliver up to justice a hundred individuals a month; whether guilty or innocent matters little to him" (III,222). He denies the charge but apparently derives satisfaction from his ability to provoke such grandiose and fantastic rumors. Seeking fame, he is yet willing to settle for notoriety; aiming to impress society, he is amenable to gaining its fear rather than its admiration. The tone of the narrative often implies as much pride in his ability to mystify people or to make them suspicious as it does annoyance at being misunderstood:

> On how many occasions have I not overwhelmed with amazement the persons who came to complain of any robbery! Scarcely had they related two or three circumstances, when I was immediately in possession of the whole facts; I concluded their story; or, without waiting for more explanations, I said, *"the thief is so and so."* They were thunderstruck; were they grateful? I think not; for generally the complainant remained persuaded either that I had committed the robbery, or that I had made a compact with the devil. (IV,14–15)

In England the *Memoirs* fell on fertile ground. In debates about the prevention and detection of crime the English had frequently turned, with both interest and suspicion, to the example of the French police. Their efficiency could be admired—in the eyes of Patrick Colquhoun, "the French system had arrived at the greatest degree of perfection"—but their involvement in political espionage only seemed to confirm traditional English fears about police forces.[5] With the movement for both penal and police reform reaching a climax at this time, it was inevitable that the memoirs of the ex-convict and ex-detective should attract widespread attention. Vidocq's fame was quickly established, and he became, in the opinion of the *Westminster Review*, "the most celebrated thief-taker that the world has known."[6]

The *Memoirs* was widely praised by the reviewers. It possessed "a good deal of piquancy and spirit" and was "certainly the most amusing production that has issued from the press of either country for many years."[7] The detective's bravado and robust good humor appealed to popular taste. The *Spectator* extolled his "vigilance, dexterity, invention, courage, humanity and integrity," while the *Literary Gazette*, only partly ironically, declared him to be "a perfect hero."[8] The perfect hero soon made his appearance on the stage. In 1829

Douglas Jerrold and John Baldwin Buckstone both wrote plays based on the *Memoirs,* bearing the same title, *Vidocq, the French Police Spy.* Jerrold's melodrama divided its two acts equally between prison and police episodes and converted the role of Vidocq into an actor's tour de force. Its second act showed how easily the French detective could be made to satisfy a public appetite for spectacle and adventure, sentiment and humor.[9]

Yet the English reaction to Vidocq, like the attitude to the French police as a whole, was ambivalent. He had succeeded in giving the detective a flair and charm that his predecessors lacked, but his tactics still offended contemporary moral sensibilities. The spectacle of the rogue in the service of the state was unsettling. The latter part of the *Memoirs,* pronounced the *Spectator* in disgust, was "nothing more than a thief-taker's memorandum-book."[10] Like Godwin before them, reviewers were alarmed at the apparently intimate relation between detection and deception. Vidocq's adventures were "a long tissue of deceit and falsehood," while their hero "at last failed in the only good quality which is sometimes found remaining in the lowest characters—that of not betraying their former companions." In all, the *Monthly Review* concluded, the French detective was "a most questionable member of society."[11] Even readers who were clearly sympathetic to detectives and not overscrupulous about their methods could be offended: "That it must frequently be necessary to use stratagem, in order to surprise bold and wary villains, and that it is lawful and laudable so to do for the protection of the honest against the dishonest, is indisputable; but those stratagems need not be of a nature to enlist all our sympathies on the side of the criminal, as Vidocq's commonly do."[12]

To contemporaries, indeed, the *Memoirs* evoked memories of Jonathan Wild. A mid-century English melodrama was actually entitled *The Thieftaker of Paris, or Vidocq! The French Jonathan Wild.*[13] Though Vidocq exonerated himself from the grosser charges of corruption, he had failed to assure contemporaries that there was a wide moral gulf separating the detective from his enemies. Wild had been both thief and thieftaker. Vidocq progresses from the one profession to the other, but it is a change of sides rather than a change of hearts, and he remains a rogue in both roles. In his memoirs, as in Wild's life, the guardian and the enemy of the law are not different figures: they are merely two expressions of the same character, different in form but disturbingly similar in content.

The considerable publicity that Vidocq's *Memoirs* received in England indicates how well the police reminiscence could answer a growing, though still ambivalent, interest in detection and detectives. Until the formation of the Criminal Investigation Department in the 1870s, England did not possess a detective force with a legendary status like the Sûreté, but popular literature turned to the Bow Street Runners, and later to the Detective Department of the Metropolitan Police, as sources of inspiration for similar fictive mélanges.

During the early part of the nineteenth century the Bow Street Runners enjoyed a number of striking, well-publicized successes.[14] In 1820, for example, they were responsible for the capture of Arthur Thistlewood, leader of the Cato Street conspiracy, while in 1823 George Ruthven, a leading Runner, arrested John Thurtell, the most famous murderer of the period. Although such triumphs testify to the Runners' efficiency as a police force, their history also makes clear that no single organization could hope to escape from the weaknesses which afflicted the police system as a whole. In the early nineteenth century there were only eight Runners, and their salary was little more than a retaining fee. Like other peace officers and other thief-takers, they were reliant on rewards and gratuities from clients. At Bow Street, the magistrate Sir Richard Birnie bluntly told a parliamentary committee, "parties must pay."[15] Apart from restricting their service to the wealthy few, this financial dependence inevitably opened the way for a familiar list of abuses. The Runners would compound felonies by negotiating private deals between thieves and their victims, a practice at which the magistrates apparently connived. No Runners were actually dismissed for corruption or charged with indictable offenses, but they approached their work with a sharp eye for personal profit, whether legal or illegal. Two of the best-known of their number, John Sayer and John Townshend, were reputed to have left suspiciously large fortunes at their deaths.[16]

Leon Radzinowicz has summed up the paradoxical nature of the organization: "The Bow Street Office soon became 'a pecuniary establishment to itself,' the headquarters of a closely knit caste of speculators in the detection of crime, self-seeking and unscrupulous, but also daring and efficient when daring and efficiency coincided with their private interest." [17] This contradiction has made the Runners' value as a police force a point of controversy among historians; but among the early nineteenth-century public the Runners' daring and efficiency appear to have attracted more notice than their love of money or lack of scruple. The Runners could be less than honest and public-spirited, but a degree of graft in most areas of public life was taken for granted. Even after the formation of similar police offices, Gilbert Armitage has written, "it was nearly always to Bow Street that application was made for the assistance of an experienced officer in the solution of obscure crimes." [18]

The Runners were not simply regarded as useful tools in the detection of crime, but achieved a popularity and prestige which had hitherto been denied to thief-takers and policemen. Their activities formed the basis of a long-lived legend, and they themselves were regarded, as Scott remarked with some irony, as "dashing heroes." [19] The tendency to lionize the Runners was encouraged by more than their daring and efficiency. The age was attracted to the odd, the eccentric, the colorful, and the men from Bow Street were noted for a flamboyance that made them the darlings of the fashionable world. John Townshend, probably the most famous of the Runners, was for many years a favorite of George III and George IV as well as a familiar figure at court and society occasions. He entered into the role of pet of the aristocracy with snobbish gusto. He proudly wore a hat that the king had given him, and on one occasion refused to intervene in a duel on the ground that the participants were not genteel enough to merit his attention. Pierce Egan invoked him in mock-heroic vein: "Thou bashaw of the *pigs* [thief-takers] and all-but *beak* [magistrate]! The satellite of kings and princes, protector of the nobility, and one of the *safeguards* of the metropolis." [20] On Townshend's death in 1832 he received an obituary in the *Gentle-*

man's Magazine, striking evidence of the reputation he had achieved.[21]

It was inevitable that Bow Street should find its way into the literature of the age. Townshend himself makes a brief appearance in Thomas Skinner Surr's *Winter in London* (1801), a popular novel dealing with fashionable society.[22] But the first novel to deal with the Runners at any length was Thomas Gaspey's *Richmond: or, Scenes in the Life of a Bow Street Officer, Drawn Up from His Private Memoranda*, published anonymously in 1827.[23] "This is at least a variety in our literature," commented a contemporary critic.[24] Anticipating Vidocq's *Memoirs* by a year, *Richmond* for the first time made a police detective the hero of the story and his work its main subject.

Originality was apparently not enough to gain public attention, and the book enjoyed a popularity as small as that of its French successor was great. It received little notice and less praise from the reviewers.[25] Showing that a distaste for detectives and for accounts of crime could be applied even to the usually popular Runners, a critic in the *Monthly Review* doubted "the capacity of the subject itself to be made attractive in any shape."[26] Readers of the age seem to have taken the *Monthly Review*'s warning: John Carter has recorded that leftover copies of the first edition were reissued in 1845 with a new title page.[27]

Richmond shows Gaspey to be a writer of technical competence—in a decade of undistinguished fiction, he was a good journeyman—but of mixed aims. The novel vacillates uneasily between the influences of Wordsworthian romanticism and the picaresque. In the portrayal of the hero, however, the picaresque triumphs, and Richmond himself is a latter-day Tom Jones. As a young man, he rebels against the job in a counting house to which his parents have consigned him and runs away to join first a company of traveling actors and then a band of gipsies.

After a while, Richmond tires of life on the open road and looks for an occupation that will guarantee him a measure of security and respectability. Gaspey had his eye resolutely on the contemporary market, so the answer to Richmond's dilemma—his desire for a job which is at once "partly regular

and partly adventurous" (I,311)—is obvious.[28] He becomes a
Bow Street Runner. The change occurs about a third of the
way through the novel, and the rest of the narrative is devoted
to an episodic account of Richmond's adventures as a detective.

The Runners enjoyed widespread sympathy and admiration,
and Gaspey's concern was to increase rather than diminish
their reputation. As an adventurer, Richmond is less of a
rogue than Vidocq: as a detective, he is both more honest and
more straightforward in his dealings. His attitude to the rewards system provides a revealing index to his character. Vidocq's zest for his work gives hints of financial self-interest, at
a time in England when the thief-taker's acceptance of blood
money was a continual cause for suspicion and dislike. At several points in the book Gaspey stresses his own hero's lack of
mercenary motives. After the trial of a body-snatcher whom he
has captured, for example, Richmond comments: "that he was
not sentenced to execution . . . eased my mind of a very dis-
agreeable feeling connected with the emoluments arising from
the capital conviction of criminals. I would much rather never
touch a guinea, than have the reflection of its being the price
of life, even though the convict had committed crimes of the
deepest dye. Forty pounds would prove but a poor recompense to me for the consciousness of having been the chief instrument in bringing a miserable wretch to the gallows" (III,
59–60).

Apart from a distaste for blood money, the passage shows a
dislike of capital punishment and a sympathy for the criminal
which reflected the growing movement for reform of the criminal law in the 1820s. Vidocq himself argues for penal reform
and from time to time shows compassion toward criminals. In
one sentimental and unlikely episode he actually accompanies
two saintly and repentant murderers to the steps of the gallows, receiving religious books and crucifixes from them as
parting gifts. Yet in general, he is too much the hunter to pay
attention to his prey's delicacies of feeling.

In Gaspey's novel the attitude has changed. The detective
not only shows greater sympathy toward the criminal but is no
longer seen solely as a criminal-catcher. He is as much the protector of the innocent and the unfortunate as the pursuer of the

guilty. Richmond does not go out looking for crimes: their victims come to him for aid, and it is his feeling for their distress which motivates his investigations. At the end of one adventure, when he returns a kidnapped child to his mother, Richmond's feelings are so far removed from those of the blood-money hunter that he receives his reward in the spirit of a medieval knight accepting a token from his mistress: "I took the purse from her agitated hand with profound obeisance; more, however, from a wish not to offend her by refusal, than from a desire for the money. The fine feelings which I had been the happy means of eliciting both towards the boy and towards myself, were an abundant reward to me. The purse, even empty, as a token of remembrance, I should have considered an ample reward" (II, 113).

Yet in becoming a Bow Street Runner, Richmond does not merely seek an opportunity for adventures, however romantic and high-minded. He also seeks a more "regular" existence than his life with the gipsies. After his enrollment with the Runners he marries, moves into modest but respectable lodgings, and settles down in earnest to the business of joining the middle classes. The process, significantly, involves not just a rejection of low life, vagrancy, and irresponsible high spirits, but also a growing criticism of the gentility and aristocracy.

Criticism of the upper classes and identification with middle-class values become the major themes of the last and longest of Richmond's adventures as a detective. The story is a little parable of the corruptions of fashionable Regency society and of the limitations of the genteel code itself. Percy, a rich young gentleman who has arrived in London fresh from the country, is quickly ensnared by a gang of aristocratic forgers and swindlers. Percy's gentility, the incident suggests, does not merely make him an easy prey for confidence men; it also makes him overscrupulous about redressing his wrongs. Richmond suffers from no such disability. "I had," he declares, "no patience with this sort of punctilio, and could have wished all the absurdities of the code of honour pitched to purgatory" (III, 284). The detective's desire for prompt and effective action elicits the reader's approval: Percy needs his money back, and the criminals need to be prevented from serving other people the same way.

The criticism of both the criminals and their victim high-lights the role of the detective. Although his work involves him in colorful adventures, it also makes him the champion of characteristically middle-class values. He becomes the scourge of crimes bred amid luxury and aristocracy. His methods, moreover, show an impatience with the intricacies of an upper-class code. Whereas Caleb Williams abandoned the code of honor in favor of a dangerous and dubious trickery, Richmond rejects "honourable prejudices" (III, 284) for what is at root the middle-class ethic of business. In his well-inten-tioned but hard-headed pragmatism, his desire to get things done with the minimum fuss, the detective is not far from the world of the Liverpool counting house which Richmond had begun by rejecting.

The Bow Street Runners survived until 1839, but shortly after the publication of Gaspey's *Richmond* their fame was overshadowed by significant changes in police administration. Bringing to a climax years of growing uneasiness about the older methods of law enforcement and finally overcoming the resistance to reform, Peel's Metropolitan Police Act of 1829 provided London with what was in effect its first real police force: a body of some eight hundred uniformed men acting under the direction of two Commissioners.

In their early years the New Police were targets for a predict-able range of criticism. Local parishes complained of the ex-pense, while the public as a whole found the police arrogant and overbearing. Particularly in radical circles, the latter ac-cusation was associated with the traditional fear that police forces were actually military bodies posing a threat to the lib-erties of the individual. Such criticism reached a climax after the police's dispersal of a radical meeting at Cold Bath Fields in 1833. A coroner's jury investigating the death of a police-man in the fracas returned a verdict of "justifiable homi-cide"—though this was later quashed—adding that the behav-ior of the police had been "ferocious, brutal, and unprovoked by the people."[29]

Yet, given the depth of traditional hostilities, the New Po-lice were accepted remarkably quickly. After 1834, Leon Rad-zinowicz has noted, "approbation was taking the place of criticism whenever it received public notice."[30] Despite some early mistakes the police handled the problem of public relations sensibly, and the public came to appreciate its presence in an era of rapidly increasing crime and frequent public disorders. "Experience has served to teach the men virtue of moderation and patience," commented a mid-century journalist, "and they are now looked upon as a constitutional force, simply because we have got accustomed to them."[31]

The Metropolitan Police was conceived primarily as a preventive rather than a detective force. The role of the constable on the beat was stressed, and in some respects the new arrangements were unfavorable to detective work. The police wore readily identifiable uniforms, and they were forbidden to frequent the pubs and flash-houses of which the Runners had long been habitués.[32] However, as recent research has shown, they did undertake detective work in their early years, and creation of the Detective Department in 1842 was not quite the act of spontaneous generation which earlier historians assumed.[33] The obscurity shrouding these early forays into detection suggests a conspiracy of silence, implying that the suspicion of the detective persisted even after the ordinary policeman had been accepted by the public. If the uniformed policeman on the beat could be disturbingly reminiscent of the soldier, the plain-clothes detective appeared perilously like the political spy.

The fear was given some color by the one well-publicized instance of police detection in the 1830s, which became a source of considerable embarrassment to the authorities. In 1831 a certain Sergeant Popay had been instructed to infiltrate a radical organization. Popay behaved like an enthusiastic and uncritical disciple of Vidocq's *Memoirs,* for he played the part of detective with tactless zeal—wearing disguise, inventing an elaborate fictitious identity for himself, and coming close to acting as an *agent provocateur.* Robert Cruikshank's pamphlet *Cruikshank v. the New Police* gave vigorous expression to the alarm aroused by the exposure of Popay's conduct in 1833. According to Cruikshank, the ideal policeman "must be as changeable as a weather-cock, and have as many different suits of clothes as there are eyes in a peacock's tail. These he must put on as occasion serves, that he may mingle, unobserved, among the people, incite them to become traitors, and then—turn INFORMER."[34] Behind specifically political fears of men like Popay lay a more general suspicion that the detective was inherently dishonest and untrustworthy, the familiar and traditional view that his work involved a breach of accepted notions of good conduct. The parliamentary committee which investigated the incident reproved Popay for "carrying concealment and deceit into the intercourse of private life."[35]

Such attitudes were deeply rooted and could survive for a long time. As late as 1869 the Commissioner of Metropolitan Police suggested that detection was "viewed with the greatest suspicion and jealousy by the majority of Englishmen and is, in fact, entirely foreign to the habits and feelings of the nation."[36] Yet as the parliamentary report on the Popay case itself demonstrated, this view was increasingly balanced by a more practical approach: the growing acknowledgment of the fact that detectives, like preventive policemen, could be both useful and necessary. During the later part of the 1830s and the early 1840s plain-clothes detectives continued to be discreetly employed, apparently under the personal direction of Richard Mayne, one of the two police Commissioners.[37] The recognition of the need for efficient detection spread gradually from the authorities to the public at large. In 1842 the initial failure of the police to capture the murderer Daniel Good, who was on the run for fifteen days and was caught only through sheer coincidence, led to widespread public concern. The outcry, led by the influential *Times,* shows a striking change in public attitudes. Twenty years before, the failure to arrest a wanted man would hardly have been worthy of notice in a *Times* editorial. But by 1842, the public already had such a taste of effective law enforcement as to demand more and better detection.

The Daniel Good case provided a timely excuse for the official establishment of a Detective Department or Office (the name varies in contemporary accounts), composed of two inspectors and six sergeants, all in plain clothes. The new department represented something less than a complete break with its predecessor, the Bow Street Runners. Organization and detective methods remained relatively unsophisticated, and the new detectives were, like the Runners, available for private hire. In one important respect, however, the new department was a distinct improvement. Although its members were hardly the paragons of virtue whom Dickens portrayed in his journalism, the department's record was for many years untainted by suspicions of corruption or sharp practice.

Although the official existence of a Detective Department reflected the growing sympathy toward police detectives, its early history shows that public attitudes remained mixed. It was established, Douglas G. Browne has pointed out "in the most unobtrusive manner," remained for many years surprisingly small (no larger than the Bow Street Runners), and its initial activities were scarcely less obscure than the earlier detective work undertaken by the Metropolitan Police. The 1840s also provided few sensational cases in which the new detectives could distinguish themselves, but it seems clear that the police authorities were content, at least in the beginning, that the department not become the focus of public attention.[38]

According to Sir Basil Thomson, the first press mention of "detective officers" being involved in a criminal case did not occur until 1845, and not until 1849 did the department achieve its first well-publicized triumph.[39] In that year several detectives—including Field and Whicher, whom Dickens was soon to meet—brought about the arrest of Frederick and Maria Manning for the murder of O'Connor, a Custom House officer. The case was widely reported, the circumstances of the murder appealing nicely to the gruesome taste of the age, and the police commissioners drew the attention of the Home Secretary to the detectives' "extraordinary exertions and skill."[40] A contemporary account of the case, Robert Huish's *The Progress of Crime, or The Authentic Memoirs of Maria Manning,* gives an admiring report of the efficiency of the police investigation, freely embellished with woodcuts showing the detectives in various dashing poses. One detail in particular impressed Huish: the use of the newly created telegraph system to post a description of the wanted couple to Edinburgh, where Maria Manning was finally caught.

From this date onward the police detectives attracted increasing publicity and, in popular literature and journalism, frequently became the objects of an admiration which verged on hero-worship. In literary terms the 1850s were dominated by the contribution of Dickens, who virtually appointed himself patron and publicist to the Detective Department. The subject appealed to both his journalist's eye for a good story and his novelist's imagination: police detectives are the subject of a series of articles published in *Household Words* and make significant appearances in his fiction. Dickens, however, was not the only writer attracted to the subject, and contrary to the common assumption, he was not the first.

Narrowly anticipating both the *Household Words* articles and *Bleak House*, *Recollections of a Detective Police-Officer*, by "Thomas Waters," first appeared in *Chambers's Edinburgh Journal* between July 1849 and September 1853. It was subsequently published in volume form in England in 1856.[41] Devoid of literary value, the *Recollections* is noteworthy for its continuation and elaboration of the traditions established by Vidocq's *Memoirs* and Gaspey's *Richmond*. Like them, the book is fiction elaborately but ineffectively masquerading as fact. The author goes to some lengths to persuade the reader of the authenticity of his adventures. The title page of the American edition identifies him as "An Inspector of the London Detective Corps," while he himself stresses that he has changed only the real names of the characters and at one point even quotes from a newspaper account of one of his cases. Such measures have succeeded in deceiving at least one historian of detective fiction, but Waters, whose real name was William Russell, was a hack novelist and journalist, not a policeman.[42]

At the time Russell was writing, the Detective Department remained small in size and the names of its members were just beginning to be made familiar to the public through press reports. It was thus perhaps to preserve his pretensions to authenticity that he dated the twelve adventures in the *Recollections* safely in the past, in the early and middle 1830s. The hero, Waters, is not a member of the Detective Department but an ordinary Metropolitan policeman, singled out by one of the Commissioners for detective work, as men like Field and Whicher had been. Yet it is obvious that Russell was attracted to the subject by the growing fame of the Detective Department. The stories have all the hallmarks of a desire to make a quick penny out of a new taste, and they belong in spirit to the late 1840s and early 1850s rather than the 1830s. Whereas earlier fictional detectives had expressed awareness of the opprobrium attached to much of their work and had sought to justify themselves, Waters contents himself with commenting that his job is "one which can scarcely be dispensed with, it seems, in this busy, scheming life of ours" (12.309; 58).[43] The brevity of the remark and its matter-of-fact air imply that greater public acceptance of the detective which characterized the mid-century.

The adventures also afford brief glimpses of an advanced state of organization among detectives more typical of the mid-century than the 1830s. Waters consults the *Police Gazette,* confers with his fellow policemen about a suspect's past life, leads a police raid on a gambling house, and is helped out in an emergency by the timely intervention of his colleagues. He even inaugurates the long literary tradition of the metropolitan officer's contempt for his rural equivalents, continued, for example, in Wilkie Collins' *The Moonstone.* Venturing into darkest Surrey on an investigation, Waters remarks complacently that the crime has "completely nonplussed the unpractised Dogberrys of the place, albeit it was not a riddle at all difficult to read" (16.306; 217).

Russell is less concerned, however, to detail the intricacies of police procedure and organization than to use the detective's work to provide his readers with entertainment and adventure according to accepted conventions. It is not surprising, therefore, that Waters is strikingly similar to both Vidocq and Richmond, his fictional predecessors. Like them, he joins the police force after a misspent youth, though in his case, as he is anxious to stress, the recklessness consisted of genteel dissipation rather than criminality. His detective methods are not those of the specialist or bureaucrat but those of the canny and experienced man of the world. He has had, as he himself boasts, "much practice in reading the faces and deportment" (16.308; 225) of his fellow men.

Waters' success depends primarily on what he archly calls his "legal metamorphoses" (14.195; 144). The *Recollections* exploits the detective's use of disguise to the point of absurdity. The hero variously appears as a Cockney dog-stealer complete with stolen dog, a "heavy and elderly, well-to-do personage" with "a flaxen wig, broad-brimmed hat, green spectacles, and a multiplicity of waistcoats and shawls" (12.117; 37–38), and a fashionable swell. On one occasion he masquerades as the wife of a suspected criminal, though admittedly with much trepidation and in a dim light. The passion for amateur theatricals has reached epidemic proportions in Russell's police force: Waters' colleagues are able to feign drunkenness at a moment's notice, with "a perfection of acting I have never seen equalled" (12.117; 40), or to transform themselves unrecognizably into Jewish moneylenders.

Vidocq's *Memoirs* had firmly established the detective's reputation as a disguise-artist, a reputation strengthened in England, as Cruikshank's pamphlet shows, by the Popay case. Although Russell is obviously indebted to this tradition and makes his hero approach detection with all the gratuitous flamboyance of a Vidocq, he also manages to rob disguise of some of its earlier pejorative associations. Vidocq's continual changeability epitomized the shadowy, impenetrable nature of his character and his love of the ethically suspect but dramatically satisfying trick. Though Waters' play-acting is associated with a belief in manipulation and stratagem, which is defended in the Preface to the 1856 edition as "legitimate . . . and . . . honourable *ruses de guerre*" (vii), he is in general devoid of his predecessor's ethic of thoroughgoing roguery.

Waters' one descent into Vidocq's amoral canniness serves to show how much the fictional detective has changed. In one adventure the hero is captured by a group of criminals intent on murdering him; he persuades Madame Duquesne, one of the less bloodthirsty members of the conspiracy, to help him escape by telling her that he can locate her missing child. In defense of the deception, Waters points to necessity and self-preservation: "I do not know, by the way, whether the falsehood I was endeavouring to palm off upon the woman was strictly justifiable or not; but I am fain to believe that there are few moralists that would not, under the circumstances, have acted pretty much as I did" (12.297; 184). Such a trick would have been all in the day's work to the French detective, an occasion for complacent commentary on his cleverness rather than for defensive remark. But Waters finds it necessary to return to the issue and to further assure himself of the reader's goodwill. The result is first to make his conduct seem more alarming and then to round off the episode with a sentimentally happy ending: "I caused Madame Duquesne to be as gently undeceived the next morning as possible, with respect to her child; but the reaction and disappointment proved too much for her wavering intellect. She relapsed into positive insanity, and was placed in Bedlam, where she remained two years. At the end of that period she was pronounced convalescent. A sufficient sum of money was raised by myself and others, not only to send her to Paris, but to enable her to set up as a milliner in a small but respectable way. As lately as last May, when I saw her there, she was in health both of mind and body, and doing comfortably" (12.297; 187–188).

Clearly, Waters is closer in temperament to the hero of Gaspey's novel than to Vidocq. The *Recollections* elaborates *Richmond's* presentation of the detective as a model of virtue and good-heartedness. The earlier novel effected an elementary redefinition of the detective's role, making him as much the defender of the weak and innocent as the nemesis of the guilty. In the *Recollections* this aspect of the detective's work has become an explicit doctrine and is stressed in the majority of the stories. Confronted in his second adventure by a murder suspect whose guilt he doubts, Waters pronounces: "My duty, I knew, was quite as much the vindication of innocence as the detection of guilt; and if I could satisfy myself that he was not the guilty party, no effort of mine should be wanting, I determined, to extricate him from the perilous position in which he stood" (12.116; 36–37). He is correct in his intuition that the accused man is innocent and successful in his efforts to capture the real culprits: "The news, late as it was, spread like wildfire, and innumerable were the congratulations which awaited me when I reached the inn where I lodged. But that which recompensed me a thousandfold for what I had done, was the fervent embrace in which the [falsely accused man's] white-haired uncle, risen from his bed to assure himself of the truth of the news, locked me, as he called down blessings from Heaven upon my head!" "There are," he concludes with more piety than irony, "blessed moments even in the life of a police-officer" (12.120; 55).

Blessed indeed, for in addition to being the friend of the unjustly accused, Waters is the good angel of the weak and helpless out-of-towner exposed to the dangerous and scheming life of the metropolis. Richmond had rescued the guileless and ineffective Percy from the clutches of forgers and gamblers, and Waters' first adventure follows essentially the same plot (it may even be directly indebted to Gaspey's novel, which was republished in 1845). In later episodes Waters continually plays the part of amateur philanthropist rather than iron agent of the criminal law. Two stories, "Mary Kingsford" and "The Widow," describe an almost identical process. In both stories a genteel heroine, innocent and defenseless, arrives alone in London and is threatened by the designs, sexual and financial, of its criminal inhabitants. Waters becomes coincidentally involved in her life out of a sense of pity and a desire to help, takes her under his care, and finally defeats her enemies.

Richmond had explicitly repudiated the image of the blood-money man and shown a compassion toward criminals which was a distant echo of the nascent social conscience of the 1820s. In Russell's work this compassion develops into a full-blown sentimentality and a belief, equally characteristic of the mid-century, in the criminal's ability to reform. When Waters is commissioned by an arrogant and snobbish city business-man to arrest a former clerk, Owen Lloyd, on a charge of theft, his sympathies flow naturally toward his prospective prey rather than his client. At one point in his investigations he reflects unhappily: "Mr. Lloyd, there could be no longer a doubt, had unconsciously betrayed his unfortunate, guilty brother into the hands of justice, and I, an agent of the iron law, was already upon the threshold of his hiding-place! I felt no pleasure at the success of the scheme." (12.311; 72). Miraculously, Owen Lloyd proves innocent and the detective is spared further laceration of his sensibilities. In a later story Waters repays a woman criminal who helps him capture a receiver of stolen goods by obtaining her pardon. At the end of the story he reports contentedly, "Several benevolent persons interested themselves in her behalf, and she was sent out to Canada, where she had some relatives, and has, I believe, prospered there" (16.311; 241).

Such sentiments were strictly in accord with the predilections of Russell's audience. In his life style, as well as his attitudes, Waters offered his middle-class public a reflection of themselves. As in *Richmond,* the detective, far from being a social pariah, is a model bourgeois hero. At the beginning of the book, however, Waters is very much the elegant and accomplished gentleman. He has been compelled to enter the police "as the sole means left me of procuring food and raiment" after a youth of "reckless follies" (12.55; 9). The status of detective, though respectable, is definitely a step down from his former position, and the change grates on him: "I was silly enough to feel somewhat nettled at the noble lady's haughtiness of manner . . . but fortunately the remembrance of my actual position, spite of my gentleman's attire, flashed vividly upon my mind; and instead of permitting my glib tongue to wag irreverently in the presence of a right honourable, I bowed with deferential acquiescence" (12.56; 13). At times he is extremely self-conscious about being a gentleman fallen on hard times. At the end of an early adventure in which he has helped unite two genteel lovers, he receives their wedding announcement and remarks with pathetic snobbery: "I was more gratified by this little act of courtesy for Emily's sake, as those who have temporarily fallen from a certain position in society will easily understand, than I should have been at the costliest present" (12.213; 80). Later he is pleased to note that the helpless woman whom he defends in "The Widow" is "refined and intellectual" (13.31; 84). His contempt for Gates, the villain of the story, is the reaction of the true gentleman to the false swell: the man's expression, he remarks, is "cunning, impudent, leering" (13.313; 84).

Waters' snobbery is less in evidence in later adventures, and the picture of his life that emerges is more lower middle-class than genteel. He adjusts to his new position in society, settling down into a comfortable and modest home life in lodgings chosen for their "cheapness and neatness" (17.259; 243). He and his wife discuss their neighbors' affairs and become involved in the lives of their fellow lodgers. One detective episode begins when they pay "a visit to Astley's, for the gratification of our youngsters, who had long been promised a sight of the equestrian marvels exhibited at that celebrated amphitheatre" (15.276; 200).

Such domestic touches are more prominent in the *Recollec-*

tions than in *Richmond,* and they play an important role in the presentation of the detective. If he ventures into a world of peril and excitement, he does so as a home-loving, family man: "At all events, whatever the danger, it was necessary to face it; and having cleaned and loaded my pistols with unusual care, and bade my wife a more than usually earnest farewell, which, by the way, rather startled her, I set off" (14.197; 160). Captured by criminals, he thinks first of home rather than escape: "A tumultuous throng of images swept confusedly past, of which the most constant and frequent were the faces of my wife and youngest child, whom I had kissed in his sleep just previous to [my] leaving home" (14.296; 177–178). Returning safely home, he is "anxious to conceal the peril I had encountered from my wife; and it was not till I had left the police force that she was informed of it" (14.297; 188).

These elements in the characterization of Waters, elaborated versions of Richmond's quiet, happy "establishment" and limited but adequate income, act as a counterpoint to the extravagance of his adventures and as a guarantee of his respectability and trustworthiness. Inhabiting a world of criminal intrigue and given to flamboyant "metamorphoses," he yet manages to remain a recognizably homely and reassuring figure: "I arrived at the lady's residence about twelve o'clock on the following day, so thoroughly disguised as a vagabond Cockney dog-stealer, that my own wife, when I entered the breakfast parlour just previous to starting, screamed with alarm and surprise" (14.196; 151–152). The elaborately skillful disguise is pure Vidocq, but the glimpse of domestic comedy is pure Bucket.

The *Recollections* was apparently successful in reaching the mass audience for which it was intended. A pirated edition of several of the early stories in the series was brought out in America in 1852.[44] Subsequently the book was translated into French and German and again issued in America, this time in an authorized edition.[45] In 1859 Russell published a sequel, and he returned to the subject in several later works: *Experiences of a French Detective Officer* (1861), "Inspector F's" *Experiences of a Real Detective* (1862), and *The Autobiography of an English Detective* (1863).

Though apparently the most prolific detective writer, Russell was not the only one to exploit so profitable a vein. From the 1850s onward the fictional detective reminiscence formed a flourishing subliterary cult, a striking evidence of the Victorian public's large and undiscriminating appetite for detective literature. Among the many later writers the pseudonymous "Andrew Forrester, Jr." was particularly active, contributing *Revelations of a Private Detective* (1863), *Secret Service, or Recollections of a City Detective* (1864), and with alarming versatility, *The Female Detective* (1864). As John Carter has pointed out this "below-stairs" tradition survived until near the end of the century, when it divided into two separate streams: "On the one side it turned to fact; on the other it joined up with that huge stream of 'bloods' which had run so strongly all through the Victorian period."[46]

The later work of Russell and his successors shows a number of changes, keeping pace with developments in the more serious detective literature of the age. With advances in police method, the detective's investigations become more scientific and orderly; his adventures thus approach closer to the detailed and ratiocinative structure of the detective short story of modern times. There is a parallel tendency to pay less attention to simple, sensational crimes and to offer miniature versions of the complex legal and familial intrigues of the three-volume novels of the day. Nevertheless, the formula which Russell had evolved out of earlier traditions usually survives as the basis of the detective's character. Like Waters, later police heroes combine exaggerated versions of Vidocq's use of disguise with Richmond's good-heartedness and adherence to middle-class values.

Russell's formula could prove successful in other genres, as Tom Taylor's popular melodrama *The Ticket-of-Leave Man* (1863) showed. The hero is Bob Brierly, a paroled convict, but the play owes much of its interest and apparently its success with Victorian audiences to the appearance of Hawkshaw, "the 'cutest detective in the force" and "the hero of the great gold dust robberies, and the famous Trunk-line-transfer forgeries." Pitted against the criminal Dalton, who has "as many outsides as he has aliases," Hawkshaw proves himself equally Protean, appearing in a new disguise for each act with an additional disguise for the finale.[47]

Taylor is determined to extract the last drop of excitement and sensation out of the business of detection, but his aim does not stop there. *The Ticket-of-Leave Man* is a fable of bourgeois morality, a Victorian counterpart to Hogarth's *Industry and Idleness*. The hero Bob Brierly, an innocent lad from Lancashire, becomes involves with the criminals Dalton and Moss and is unjustly accused and convicted of one of their crimes. After his release on parole as a "ticket-of-leave man," he is determined to achieve a respectable niche in city business but is again approached by Dalton and Moss, anxious to lure him into crime. What follows is essentially a battle for Bob's soul between the forces of evil, represented by the criminal underworld with its easy pleasures and easy money, and the forces of good, epitomized by Bob's long-suffering wife and his employer's office in the City.

Hawkshaw's involvement in the process is revealing, for he becomes Bob's good angel, just as Dalton and Moss are his bad angels. Though originally responsible for Bob's arrest and convinced of his guilt for much of the action, the detective is sympathetic to the paroled convict ("Poor devil, he's paid his debt at Portland") and anxious to help him lead an honest life. In a predictable climax Hawkshaw proves Bob's innocence and brings his temptors to justice. By his agency Bob has been firmly placed on the straight and narrow path of mid-Victorian virtue, guided by the motto "Be Steady—stick to work and home," and inspired by his employer's promise, "In the City there's no gap between the first round of the ladder and the top of the tree."[48]

Taylor's portrait of Hawkshaw represents the apotheosis of the police detective in mid-Victorian literature and illustrates with a paradigmatic clarity the change that his reputation has undergone. Earlier, in the work of Defoe and Harrison Ainsworth, Jonathan Wild had appeared as the corrupter and destroyer of innocence and youth in the big city. Here, for all the extravagance of his methods, the detective is very like the Victorian philanthropist. In the complex and perilous world of the metropolis he acts as the defender of embattled innocence

and champion of the dominant social morality. The characterization, common in the age, neatly fulfills the double function
of mass literature, offering both fantastic adventure and reassuring didacticism. Yet the importance of Waters, Hawkshaw,
and their fictional colleagues is not wholly confined to popular
literature: they are the crude substructure on which Dickens'
immeasurably more sophisticated achievement is based.

II

THE MID-VICTORIANS

As the paper-chase is the most glorious pursuit undertaken by boys, as fox-hunting is the sport of sports for men, so man hunting is the avocation fitted for heroes.
        —James Payn, *Lost Sir Massingberd* (1864)

Once more, let me say, I am thankful I live in the days of the Detective Police; if I am murdered, or commit bigamy,—at any rate, my friends will have the comfort of knowing all about it.
        —Anon., "Disappearances," *Household Words* (1851)

4
Charles Dickens

In the first half of the nineteenth century popular literature, keeping in step with developments in social history, portrayed the detective in an increasingly sympathetic manner. With the publication of Waters' *Recollections* a definite stereotype of the police detective emerged, and he was established as a popular hero whose character reflected the values of a predominantly middle-class reading public. In the middle years of the century this figure reappeared with only minor variations in a succession of "yellowbacks," predecessors of today's pulp crime fiction, and in stage melodramas. The period, however, is notable mainly for the adaptation of the stereotype to the conventions of the three-volume novel or the lengthy magazine serial.

This interest in the detective is particularly evident in the work of the "sensation novelists," as the exponents of the popular school of fiction pioneered by Dickens were usually called. The sensation novel adapted the interests which had characterized the earlier schools of Gothic and Newgate fiction to the taste of the Victorian middle-class public and to the requirements of magazine serialization. Eschewing psychological analysis, sensation fiction used techniques which invite comparison with contemporary stage melodrama; it showed a preference for the striking and unusual situation or series of events and for characters in the grip of strong or extreme emotion. Correspondingly, it aimed to provoke a strong but usually simple emotional response from the reader; like the Gothic fiction from which it derived, it was based primarily on the appeal to fear. At the same time, this love of the unusual was combined with an interest in fact and topicality, in creating an air of contemporary verisimilitude. Characteristically, the sensation novelist aimed to produce, in Walter C. Phillips' phrase, "a romance of the here and now."[1]

It is not difficult to see why the sensation novel proved so congenial a form in which to express the newly awakened enthusiasm for detectives. Since crime provides almost endless opportunities for the introduction of startling ingredients and displays of passion, it was inevitably a staple ingredient of the sensation novelists' work. By using the police detective, they were able to infuse a note of topicality into the handling of an old and time-worn subject. In the 1850s and 1860s the Detective Department was still regarded as an intriguing innovation, a sign of the changing times, and was still attracting widespread publicity in the popular press and elsewhere. In adapting to fictional purposes the contemporary or near-contemporary crimes in which police investigation had played a prominent role, the sensation novelists achieved their most satisfying blend of romance and fact. The Manning case is echoed in *Bleak House*, while the Constance Kent case gave Wilkie Collins several hints for the plot of *The Moonstone*. Palmer and Pritchard, the poisoners, and Charles Peace, the burglar and murderer, quickly found their way into the sensation fiction of the age.

The introduction of the detective into such accounts does not merely provide an old subject with a topical twist; it also reassures the reader of the writer's moral bias. In earlier Newgate fiction an interest in crime had led to an almost exclusive concentration on the criminal himself, and the result was, at least in the eyes of a majority of contemporaries, morally dubious. The work of Lytton and Ainsworth, critics had charged, made the criminal a dangerously sympathetic and glamorous figure. Although a vein of latent sympathy for the criminal runs through much sensation fiction—Dickens is at once the most striking and most complex example—writers were on the whole determined to stay on safer ground than their predecessors and to avoid ruffling the tender moral sensibilities of their audience. By presenting the policeman sympathetically, the writer implicitly allied himself with accepted social standards; and the policeman's presence helped assure a denouement in which the good would end well and the bad badly.

Sensation novels, however, are rarely concerned solely with crime and are hardly "crime stories" in the literal sense of the term. Characteristically they create a pervasive air of mystery to which mysterious crime is merely one contributing factor. Mystery does not take the form of those abstract and quasi-mathematical problems of Poe's Dupin tales or of much modern detective fiction. It arises instead out of confusions in human relationships. Sensation fiction presents a world of missing wills, long-lost heirs, mistaken identities, relatives who disappear to be reunited with their families in the final volume or installment, and illegitimate children who live in ignorance of their true parentage.

Dickens' contribution is basic to the development of both the sensation novel in general and the stereotype of the detective in particular. His persistent interest in crime, mystery, and detection culminates in *Bleak House,* in which the policeman Inspector Bucket plays a vital role. Two earlier works also figure importantly in the background to the handling of detection in *Bleak House: Martin Chuzzlewit* and a series of articles written for *Household Words* setting forth Dickens' views on the Detective Department.

Despite his pervasive interest in crime, Dickens introduces detectives into his earliest fiction only briefly. Blathers and Duff, the Bow Street Runners called to investigate Sikes' attempted burglary of the Maylies' house in *Oliver Twist,* are present for only a few pages of the action and are used simply to provide a comic interlude. When detection is necessary to the progress of a plot or to the culmination of a story, this function is sketchily and hastily attached to the role of one of the main characters, to Mr. Brownlow in *Oliver Twist* and Reuben Haredale in *Barnaby Rudge.*

Not until *Martin Chuzzlewit* does Dickens present a serious or sustained portrait of a detective. Jonas Chuzzlewit's murders, which provide the book's main subplot, are brought to light through the activities of Nadgett, an employee of the Anglo-Bengalee Disinterested Loan and Life Insurance Company, "the man at a pound a week who made the inquiries" (27.451).[2] Nadgett's particular professional status was no doubt suggested to Dickens by his source for much of the Jonas Chuzzlewit plot: the case of Thomas Griffiths Wainewright, the poisoner whose crimes were discovered in 1835 as the result of investigations made by his victims' insurance companies.[3]

The effect of Nadgett's actions is to ally him with the "good party" in the book. He helps the two Martins, Mark Tapley, John Westlock, and Tom Pinch defeat the villain, Jonas. Yet he is presented as a necessary evil rather than a force for good. From his first appearance he cuts an unsympathetic, unprepossessing figure: "a short, dried-up, withered, old man . . .

He was mildewed, threadbare, shabby; always had flue upon his legs and back" (27.451).

 Martin Chuzzlewit was published in 1843–1844, and in this respect it clearly echoes the attitude to detectives current before the Detective Department had made a favorable impact on public opinion. Nadgett is made to appear sinister in ways that echo the popular views of Wild and Vidocq. His actions are given an aura of criminality. On his first appearance he closes the door of his employer's office "as carefully as if he were about to plot a murder" (27.451), and he later rings the doorbell "in a covert under-handed way, as though it were a treasonable act" (38.595). His work has overtones of diabolism. Jonas' murder of Montague Tigg is described as a descent into hell—"Then he went down, down, down, into the dell" (47.728)—and at times the detective seems to be not so much the discoverer of Jonas' guilt as the agent of his damnation. Seemingly harmless in Jonas' eyes, Nadgett is in reality his "watchful enemy" (51.791); he appears "as if he had that moment come up a trap" (38.595); and he enters Jonas' name "over and over again" in his "great pocket-book" (38.593). When he points at the murderer, he looks "like the Tempter in some grim old carving" (40.632). In the scene where Jonas is finally confronted with his crimes, Nadgett's manner is that of Mephistopheles coming to claim his own rather than of the bringer of truth and light.

Vidocq's *Memoirs* had shown how the detective could be an impenetrable, mysterious figure, and Nadgett himself is a "man of mystery" (38.593) in more senses than one: "It was no virtue or merit in Nadgett that he transacted all his Anglo-Bengalee business secretly and in the closest confidence; for he was born to be a secret . . . How he lived was a secret; where he lived was a secret; and even what he was, was a secret" (27.451). This secrecy is useful to his job, for it disarms suspicion, "suggesting, not that he was watching any one, but that he thought some other man was watching him" (38.594). But it is more an innate psychological condition than a professional ploy. When he concludes that Jonas killed Anthony Chuzzlewit, Nadgett does not make the matter public but takes it to Tigg, confessing: "It almost takes away any pleasure I may have had in this inquiry even to make it known to you"

(38_98). In the scene where the detective accuses Jonas of
Tig_s murder, Dickens is careful to note: "The ruling passion
of _e man expressed itself even then, in the tone of regret in
wh_n he deplored the approaching publicity of what he
kn_" (51.793).

_dgett is presented as a typical specimen of the book's
u_n milieu: "he belonged to a class; a race peculiar to the
ci_who are secrets as profound to one another, as they are to
th_st of mankind" (27.452). The detective's secretiveness is
th_xtreme embodiment of that selfishness with which *Martin
C_lewit* is concerned. In his obsessive desire to keep the
s_nviolate Nadgett has merely distorted and destroyed it.
L_many of the other characters in the book, he com-
r_cates with the world around him through a series of de-
l_tely misleading personae: "In his musty old pocket-book
_rried contradictory cards, in some of which he called
_lf a coal-merchant, in others a wine-merchant, in others
_mission-agent, in others a collector, in others an accoun-
_s if he really didn't know the secret himself" (27.451).

_result in Nadgett's case is a condition of lifeless decay—
_"dried-up" and seems "to have secreted his very blood"
_1)—and a complete isolation. Despite his knowledge of
_people, the detective can communicate with nobody.
_s describes his methods of spying and of noting down
_ce in two revealing metaphors:

_vas always keeping appointments in the City, and the
_r man never seemed to come . . . He carried bits of
_ng-wax and a hieroglyphical old copper seal in his
_et, and often secretly indited letters in corner-boxes
_e trysting-places before mentioned; but they never
_red to go to anybody, for he would put them in a
_place in his coat, and deliver them to himself weeks
_ards, very much to his own surprise, quite yellow.
_1–452)

_h Dickens' unsympathetic presentation of the detec-
_ted in contemporary popular attitudes, it also
_ore serious concerns which his later fiction de-
_detection is again firmly located in the
_nvolve a combination of
secretiveness and inquisitiveness which can ultimately lead to

spiritual death. The character of the lawyer Tulkinghorn, in particular, is to a large extent an elaboration of the earlier portrait of Nadgett. Yet at the same time Dickens' attitude to professional detectives changed considerably in the years between *Martin Chuzzlewit* and *Bleak House*. For although Nadgett strongly resembles Tulkinghorn, he is completely unlike the jovial and likable Inspector Bucket. This change is seen both in Dickens' life and in his journalism during the late 1840s and early 1850s, when he developed an enthusiastic interest in the newly created Detective Department and made it the subject of a series of eulogistic articles published in *Household Words*.

During the 1840s Dickens followed contemporary criminal cases with his usual close attention. He attended the executions of Benjamin Courvoisier, the servant who murdered Lord William Russell, and of the Mannings, and his letters and journalism reveal a familiarity with several of the decade's other famous criminals, such as Henry Hocker, the Hampstead murderer, and James Blomfield Rush, the Norfolk farmer convicted of killing two of his neighbors. At this time his interest in criminal matters centered on the problem of capital punishment. But several of the cases that raised the issue also gave considerable publicity to the work of the police, and this aspect did not escape Dickens' notice. Visiting the scene of Rush's crime in 1849, he was interested, though unimpressed, by the police investigation; the search for the murder weapon, he wrote in a letter to John Forster, was being conducted in a "consummately stupid" manner.[4]

With police and detectives becoming more and more newsworthy by the end of the decade, it was logical that Dickens' interest should find expression in his newly formed magazine *Household Words*. During the years 1850–1853 he published a number of articles by himself and his colleagues dealing with police work in general and detection in particular. The series was started by W. H. Wills, the magazine's co-editor, with a piece entitled "The Modern Science of Thief-Taking," describing the organization of the Detective Department. Between July and September of 1850 Dickens wrote "A Detective Police Party" (in two parts) and "Three Detective Anecdotes," both articles being the result of meetings in the magazine office with most of the staff of detectives. In 1851, in "On Duty with Inspector Field," Dickens described a nocturnal tour of the London slums made under Field's guidance, and in 1853, in "Down with the Tide," he presented the results of a similar on-the-spot observation of the Thames River Police. Meanwhile, he and Wills collaborated on "The Metropolitan Protectives," an account of the night work of the London police stations. Other relevant material published in the magazine during this period included a comparison of the French and English police forces, to the great advantage of the latter, and a desultory correspondence about mysterious disappearances.[5]

Dickens' contact with the police extended beyond his work as a journalist. In particular he appears to have struck up a casual and intermittent acquaintance with Inspector Field, head of the Detective Department and probably the best-known detective of the middle years of the century. When producing Bulwer-Lytton's play *Not So Bad As We Seem* in 1850 at the Duke of Devonshire's house, he hired Field to prevent a threatened intrusion into the theater by Rosina, Lytton's estranged and deranged wife. "He is discretion itself," Dickens assured the Duke about Field, "and accustomed to the most delicate missions" (*Letters* II,306).[6] A letter written to Angela Burdett-Coutts in 1852, which speaks of Field's "horrible sharpness," makes clear that Dickens was still in occasional contact with the detective.[7]

The detective articles, like most of Dickens' journalism, are impressionistic and unstatistical in the extreme. In the account of the meetings at the *Household Words* office the scene is briefly set and the detectives are introduced under whimsical and transparent *noms de guerre*. Inspector Field becomes Wield, for example, and Sergeant Whicher, Witchem. The reader is given thumbnail sketches of their appearance and personalities: Inspector Stalker is "a shrewd, hard-headed Scotchman—in appearance not at all unlike a very acute, thoroughly-trained schoolmaster, from the Normal Establishment at Glasgow," while Witchem has "something of a reserved and thoughtful air, as if he were engaged in deep arithmetical calculations" (150–151). Dickens is especially concerned to capture the characteristic speech mannerisms of his subjects. Wield continually punctuates his conversation with the phrase, "Because the reason why? I'll tell you" (e.g. 151).

This groundwork laid, the remainder of the articles is devoted to accounts by the detectives of their most interesting cases. These anecdotes fall into a conventional pattern. Although Wills's article had mentioned the detectives' involvement in "family mysteries, the investigation of which demands the utmost delicacy and tact," they are shown enjoying picaresque adventures in the world of criminal low life.[8] They mingle with the "swell mobs" and pursue petty criminals with names like Tally-ho Thompson. Their methods are acting, disguise, and trickery. Sergeant Straw has the gift of impersonating "any mild character you choose to prescribe to him, from a charity-boy upwards" (151). Sergeant Mith recounts a case in which he played the part of a butcher: "Even while he spoke, he became a greasy, sleepy, shy, good-natured, chuckle-headed, unsuspicious, and confiding young butcher. His very hair seemed to have suet in it, as he made it smooth upon his head, and his fresh complexion to be lubricated by large quantities of animal food" (160). Trying to catch a suspect unawares, Wield arranges an elaborate charade in which he pretends to be selling the man a horse: " 'There, sir!' I says. 'There's a neat thing!' 'It ain't a bad style of thing,' he says. 'I believe you,' says I. 'And there's a horse!'—for I saw him looking at it. 'Rising Eight!' I says, rubbing his fore-legs. (Bless you, there ain't a man in the world knows less of horses than I do, but I'd heard my friend at the Livery Stables say he was eight year old, so I says, as knowing as possible, 'Rising Eight.')" (158–159).

Dickens was usually acutely skeptical of the claims that public officials made for themselves. He was also an experienced journalist, and such journalists are commonly suspicious of subjects too anxious to provide them with good copy. The tone of admiration, often of naive and uncritical admiration, which permeates his articles therefore comes as a surprise: "They sit down in a semi-circle (the two Inspectors at the two ends) at a little distance from the round table, facing the editorial sofa. Every man of them, in a glance, immediately takes an inventory of the furniture and an accurate sketch of the editorial presence. The Editor feels that any gentleman in company could take him up, if need should be, without the smallest hesitation, twenty years hence" (150). Passages like this, which is far from atypical, convince the reader not that Field and his colleagues are impressive men but that Dickens is determined to be impressed by them. The detectives are presented as prodigies of a marvelous calm efficiency, all-knowing and all-powerful—possessors, to borrow Philip Collins' term, of a magical "omnicompetence."[9] Dickens establishes the keynote at the beginning of the first article with the assertion that the new force "is so well chosen and trained, proceeds so systematically and quietly, does its business in such a workmanlike manner, and is always so calmly and steadily engaged in the service of the public, that the public really do not know enough of it, to know a tithe of its usefulness" (149).

The intensity of Dickens' admiration has provoked comment. George Augustus Sala, a witness of the meetings in the editorial office, later remarked that Dickens overestimated Field's intelligence; he found the novelist's love of the police "curious and almost morbid."[10] Humphry House has cited Dickens' "almost fanatical devotion" to the police as evidence of a "strong authoritarian strain" in his character.[11] Collins has made a thorough investigation of Dickens' "boyish hero-worship" of the police.[12]

The police force would have been especially attractive to a man of Dickens' social sympathies. Despite the increasingly radical nature of his disillusion with contemporary society, he did not waver in his belief that the present was an improvement on the past. "If I ever destroy myself," he exclaimed in 1843, "it will be in the bitterness of hearing those infernally and damnably good old times extolled."[13] He saw the past as a saga of Tory muddle and cruelty and found its supreme achievement in the Bloody Code and the older system of law enforcement. Inevitably, therefore, the establishment of centrally organized police and detective forces was to him a welcome development. In fact, the detectives represented a new social idea. Drawn from the lower but still respectable classes of society, they belonged to an organization which had been founded in the face of traditionalist prejudice and which relied on a democratic system of promotion rather than on the jobbery that riddled the older bureaucracies. In this respect, Dickens' love of the police stemmed from the same impulses that made him admire the working-class inventor Daniel Doyce and attack the nepotistical Barnacles in *Little Dorrit*.

There is, however, another side to Dickens' admiration of the detectives. He does not simply glorify them as paragons of efficiency and hard work; he is also unduly impressed by the air of raffish adventure with which they endowed their work. At this time Dickens was himself becoming discontented with his own respectability; he was beginning to travel restlessly and to seek the company of the Bohemian Wilkie Collins. There was much about the detectives' lives to appeal to his appetite for something beyond the confines of middle-class existence, as the article "On Duty with Inspector Field" makes clear. Here both social conscience and a spirit of sociological inquiry are almost wholly in abeyance to a rather juvenile quest for adventure and excitement. Field could usher Dickens into an alien and faintly exotic world associated with crime and mystery, which formed a refreshing contrast to his daytime life as a respected novelist and father of a rapidly expanding family.

Field and his fellow detectives expressed their own love of adventure in the same way that Dickens did, by an elaborate indulgence in acting and disguise. The novelist had always been attracted to the stage, and by the early 1850s amateur theatricals had become one of the chief outlets for that restless energy which his ordinary life could not satisfy. In the same year that he began to eulogize the work of the detectives he was also playing the part of Gabblewig in a farce which he had written with Mark Lemon, requiring "five or six changes of face, voice, and gait." [14] If nothing else, the interviews at the *Household Words* office were a meeting of hams.

The detective articles and Dickens' personal contact with Field are both relevant to *Bleak House*. In that novel Inspector Bucket inherits most of the characteristics ascribed to his real-life counterparts. In particular, as contemporaries noted, Inspector Field seems to have provided much of the raw material out of which the fictional portrait grew. [15] In physique and mannerisms Bucket is directly reminiscent of Field, who in the person of Wield is described in the first article as "a middle-aged man of a portly presence, with a large, moist, knowing eye, a husky voice, and a habit of emphasising his conversation by the aid of a corpulent forefinger, which is constantly in juxta-position with his eyes or nose" (150).

Two further parallels connect the fictional and real detectives. The night spent observing Field amid the slums of London provides the basis for the scene in *Bleak House* where Inspector Bucket conducts the surprised and bewildered Mr. Snagsby to Tom-All-Alone's. Also, Inspector Field had worked on the Manning case, though not in a prominent capacity; and it was to Maria Manning that Dickens turned for his portrait of Mademoiselle Hortense, whom Inspector Bucket arrests for the murder of Tulkinghorn.[16]

Yet is is rash to assume that the treatment of the police detective in *Bleak House* is simply an extension of the uncritical hero-worship revealed in the journalism. *Martin Chuzzlewit* had already shown that Dickens was fully aware of the sinister aspects of detection. As elaborated in *Bleak House*, the themes of *Martin Chuzzlewit* provide a controlling and defining context—the sort of context that the journalism lacks—for the handling of Inspector Bucket. In this respect, as in so many others, Dickens' fiction reveals an intelligence and subtlety for which neither his journalism nor his private life fully prepares the reader.

When John Ruskin, in his essay on "Fiction, Fair and Foul," wished to illustrate the morbid craving for excitement that "marks the peculiar tone of the modern novel"—the appetite, in fact, for sensation fiction—the book which came first to mind was *Bleak House*.[17] The modern reader finds it difficult to view the novel as an example of the decadence of Victorian taste, but Ruskin's underlying point can hardly be denied. For *Bleak House* is the sensation novel par excellence. The plot, with its profusion of missing wills, guilty secrets, and dispersed families, is a comprehensive index to the conventions of the genre.

Yet these mysteries are not merely contrivances designed to excite and entertain; they are vehicles for the analysis of a fragmenting culture. *Bleak House*, Edmund Wilson has suggested, belongs to a genre of which Dickens is the sole exponent, "the detective story which is also a social fable."[18] The novel anatomizes a society which, though deeply interconnected, lives largely in ignorance, denial, or neglect of its connecting links. The point is implicit in the elaborate topographical description with which the book opens. As J. Hillis Miller has noted, the fog has a double effect on the city landscape which it pervades.[19] On the one hand, it acts as a cohesive presence, binding together the various constituents of the scene into a paralyzed and moribund unity. On the other hand, the fog fragments the landscape. Connections are obscured, and people exist as single and apparently unrelated units: "Chance people on the bridges peeping over the parapets into a nether sky of fog, with fog all round them, as if they were up in a balloon, and hanging in the misty clouds" (1.1).

The novel then introduces a series of apparently unrelated social milieus, each one a separate and self-enclosed world. There is the muddled and inefficient Court of Chancery, especially that part of it connected with the interminable case of Jarndyce versus Jarndyce. Its hangers-on include mistreated and crazed suitors like Miss Flite and Gridley, the man from Shropshire, and neighbors like Krook, the second-hand dealer, and Snagsby, the law stationer. There is the world of high society, centering on the haughty Sir Leicester and Lady Dedlock and their family lawyer, the sinister Tulkinghorn. There is the world of the poor, which includes Nemo, the obscure legal copyist, Jo, the illiterate crossing-sweeper, and Mr. George, the happy-go-lucky ex-soldier who runs a shooting gallery. And finally, there is Bleak House itself, where John Jarndyce, turning his back on the lawsuit that bears his name, has attempted to create an oasis of peace and order. He acts as the guardian of an artificial family composed of Esther Summerson, the novel's heroine, and Richard Carstone and Ada Clare, two wards of the Court of Chancery.

The narrative method is designed to show the underlying coherence of these disparate groups. This is most evident in the plot of which Esther Summerson is the heroine. Beginning life in the home of the cold and vindictive Miss Barbary, Esther is encouraged to believe herself an orphan of obscure parentage. Later, when she has joined Jarndyce's household, she realizes that she is the illegitimate daughter of Lady Dedlock. At the end of the novel, she discovers that her father was Nemo, who had been Lady Dedlock's lover before her marriage. The revelation that the fashionable lady, the obscure orphan, and the legal copyist are all connected by familial bonds is symbolic. In spite of itself, the society of *Bleak House* forms a single unit, a "community in error, guilt, and responsibility."[20]

But this realization is largely denied to the characters themselves. From their restricted viewpoint, bewildering variety is more apparent than unity of coherence. "We both grub on in a muddle" (5.52), says Krook of himself and his spiritual brother, the Lord Chancellor. They, like most of the characters, live surrounded by perplexities which they can never properly understand. Mr. Snagsby, the epitome of the harmless little man, is involved in mysteries "of which he is a partaker, yet in which he is not a sharer" (32.443): "Mr. Snagsby cannot make out what it is he has had to do with. Something is wrong, somewhere; but what something, what may come of it, to whom, when, and from which unthought of and unheard of quarter, is the puzzle of his life" (25.352).

The characteristic response to this pervasive confusion which continually threatens to engulf the individual is not passive. A large number of the characters in *Bleak House* seek, in Miller's words, "some kind of clarity, some knowledge about themselves or about one another, some revelation of a mystery," and it is from this activity that much of the plot arises.[21] Inhabiting a milieu where disorder and lack of connection perpetually create mysteries, they become detectives.

Esther Summerson remarks of her childhood self: "I had always rather a noticing way—not a quick way, O no!—a silent way of noticing what passed before me, and thinking I should like to understand it better" (3.15). Her inquisitiveness is closely related to compassion: "my comprehension is quickened when my affection is" (3.16). The desire to know more about people is part of her struggle to escape from the chilly isolation in which she has been brought up by Miss Barbary.

This attitude represents an ideal of good detection against which the activities of the book's other detectives are judged. However, as the action develops, Esther's curiosity becomes severely modified, though her compassionate instincts are continually displayed. She cultivates an indifference toward the mystery of her own origins, telling Jarndyce that there is "nothing in the world" (8.98) that she wishes to know about herself. And she discourages the attempts by Guppy, a lawyer's clerk, to discover the relationship between her and Lady Dedlock. Later, the dreams that hint at this relationship come as a painful and unwelcome experience: "Dare I hint at that worse time when, strung together in great black space, there was a flaming necklace, or ring, or starry circle of some kind, of which I was one of the beads! And when my only prayer was to be taken off from the rest, and when it was such inexplicable agony and misery to be part of the dreadful thing?" (35.487). This deliberate lack of curiosity about her birth is partly an expression of Esther's habit of self-effacement and self-sacrifice. But in a broader sense it is also an expression of the values represented by Bleak House, the home of which she becomes the domestic goddess; it echoes Jarndyce's own indifference to the baffling intricacies of the lawsuit to which he is a party. Though the inhabitants of Bleak House make charitable forays into the society around them, they live to a large extent detached from its perplexities. Despite their social concerns, their main value is that of cultivating their own garden, attempting to create order and family harmony in retreat from the surrounding confusion.

Nevertheless, in the world outside Bleak House the impulse to detection is everywhere apparent. The peace of Jarndyce's and Esther's sanctuary itself is disrupted by the intrusion of Coavinses, the debt-collecting "follerer" who "never tired of watching" (15.207), and of Guppy, the lawyer's clerk who yearns to try his legal skills on the problem of Esther's parentage; and its harmony is destroyed by Richard Carstone's determination to get at "the core of that mystery" (23.318), the case of Jarndyce versus Jarndyce.

The role of even a minor figure like Mrs. Snagsby is devoted almost entirely to the expression of a compulsive curiosity about the relation—though in fact entirely innocent—between her husband and Jo, the crossing-sweeper. Her inquisitiveness impels her to "nocturnal examinations of Mr. Snagsby's pockets; to secret perusals of Mr. Snagsby's letters;

to private researches in the Day Book and Ledger, till, cash-box, and iron safe; to watchings at windows, listenings behind doors, and a general putting of this and that together by the wrong end" (25.353). Mr. Snagsby is inclined to take a lenient, if nervous, view of his wife's detection and to ascribe a therapeutic function to it: "Poor little thing," he tells Tulkinghorn, "she's liable to spasms, and it's good for her to have her mind employed" (22.304). But it is clear to the reader that Mrs. Snagsby's spying begins in neurotic obsession and ends in dangerous fantasy:

> Mrs. Snagsby screws a watchful glance on Jo, as he is brought into the little drawing-room by Guster. He looks at Mr. Snagsby the moment he comes in. Aha! Why does he look at Mr. Snagsby? Mr. Snagsby looks at him. Why should he do that, but that Mrs. Snagsby sees it all? Why else should that look pass between them, why else should Mr. Snagsby be confused, and cough a signal cough behind his hand? It is as clear as crystal that Mr. Snagsby is that boy's father. (25.355)

Mrs. Snagsby's final, ludicrous deduction is a comic echo of the solution to the book's main mystery plot, the relation between Lady Dedlock and Esther.[22] In fact, her role provides a burlesque of the more serious types of detection which that mystery provokes, especially the actions of Krook and Tulkinghorn. In them, as in Mrs. Snagsby, the detective impulse is a negative rather than a positive force. Their spying echoes that of Nadgett in *Martin Chuzzlewit*: divorced from any of Esther's compassionate instincts, it perpetuates rather than cures the malaise of the society, and it hinges upon a sterile combination of inquisitiveness and secretiveness.

In the earlier novel Nadgett's possession of information about his fellows was epitomized by his pocketbook, bulging untidily with private notes and memoranda. In the character of Krook the desire to understand and control the surrounding environment is identified almost entirely with the instinct to acquire and hoard physical possessions. "All's fish that comes to my net" (5.25), Krook tells Esther when she first enters his shop. He presides over a random assortment of "Magpie property" (62.835) in which rubbish and useless articles are mixed with the missing will that is the key to Jarndyce versus Jarndyce and the letters that prove the connection between Lady Dedlock and Nemo. Furtive and distrustful, Krook's attitude to his environment is predatory. He collects human hair, even having designs on Ada Clare's at one point, and cat skins, while his cat, the emblem of himself, passes its time stalking Miss Flite's birds. The property that Krook acquires is never released or distributed: his is a shop where everything is bought and nothing is sold.

The result is both sterile and fatal. Krook never achieves control or power over others, for he can neither order nor understand what he collects. At the beginning of the book he cannot even read the documents in his possession, and when he does try to learn, his lodger Weevle reports: "He can make all the letters separately, and he knows most of them separately when he sees them . . . but he can't put them together" (32.448). Like the letters on the page, Krook's collection is a matter merely of unrelated multiplicity, the exaggeration of rather than the opposite of the disorder and lack of coherence in the world outside his shop. Unable to assimilate what he ingests, Krook can only go on ingesting until he destroys himself.

While Krook's shop is a receptacle for physical possessions, Tulkinghorn is himself a "silent depository" for secrets and "family confidences" (2.11).[23] His inquiries into Lady Dedlock's past are not a pursuit of truth for its own sake but a pursuit of truth for the power that it brings its sole possessor. He has the instincts of the blackmailer and is motivated by the desire to manipulate other people. As the lawyer awaits his final interview with Lady Dedlock, the narrator comments: "To say of a man so severely and strictly self-repressed that he is triumphant, would be to do him as great an injustice as to suppose him troubled with love or sentiment, or any romantic weakness. He is sedately satisfied. Perhaps there is a rather increased sense of power upon him, as he loosely grasps one of his veinous wrists with his other hand, and holding it behind his back walks noiselessly up and down" (41.573). Through both the third-person narrative and the first-person account of Esther Summerson's life, Dickens is concerned to insist that those values, "love or sentiment, or any romantic weakness," to which Tulkinghorn's desire for power is opposed, form the only basis for true connections between people and a true social order. In this sense, the difference between Krook's failure and Tulkinghorn's success at detection hardly matters. Though Tulkinghorn uncovers the real relationship between Lady Dedlock, Nemo, and Esther, his use of that knowledge—to convert himself into exploiter and Lady Dedlock into victim—merely echoes one of the major social divisions besetting the world of *Bleak House*.

Harmful to others, his detection proves of little use to himself. His inquiries cause Mademoiselle Hortense, Lady Dedlock's maid, to murder him; but even before that Tulkinghorn exists in a state of life-in-death. His inquisitiveness about others is matched by a constitutional secretiveness about himself: he is "a hard-grained man, close, dry and silent" (22.303) and "an Oyster of the old school, whom nobody can open" (10.130). Like Krook and Nadgett, he takes in everything he can and gives nothing back to the surrounding world: "Mute, close, irresponsive to any glancing light, his dress is like himself" (2.11). The absence of a reciprocal relationship with anything outside himself leads to lifeless isolation. He is divorced from both human contact and human experience, "dwelling among mankind but not consorting with them, aged without genial youth" (42.582). He is shown throughout in mute and static poses. Commonly he is described sitting alone in his chambers amid images of dust and rust, as well as more explicit reminders of death:

> More impenetrable than ever, he sits, and drinks, and mellows as it were, in secrecy; pondering, at that twilight hour . . . that one bachelor friend of his, a man of the same mould and a lawyer too, who lived the same kind of life until he was seventy-five years old, and then, suddenly conceiving (as it is supposed) an impression that it was too monotonous, gave his gold watch to his hairdresser one summer evening, and walked leisurely home to the Temple and hanged himself. (22.304)

The novel's general preoccupation with mystery, the appearance of several minor detectives like Mrs. Snagsby, and the presentation in Esther Summerson, on the one hand, and in Krook and Tulkinghorn, on the other, of two radically different approaches to detection provide a context which lends importance to the role of the policeman, Inspector Bucket. His participation in the action is relatively small: he is not introduced until about a third of the way through the novel and he is present in only nine of its sixty-seven chapters. But he is involved in several plots and subplots, and is the most explicit articulation of the book's interest in detection and detectives. Acting on Tulkinghorn's behalf, Inspector Bucket tracks down Jo, who unknowingly holds vital evidence about Lady Dedlock's past. Again acting as the lawyer's agent, the policeman serves a warrant on Gridley for contempt of the Court of Chancery. After the murder of Tulkinghorn, Bucket arrests first, mistakenly, Mr. George and then, correctly, Mademoiselle Hortense. When Lady Dedlock runs away from her husband in shame at the exposure of her past, the policeman takes Esther Summerson with him and tries to track the missing woman down, eventually discovering her body by the graveyard where Nemo, her ex-lover, has recently been buried. Bucket also deals with a group of minor villains—the miserly Grandfather Smallweed, the hypocritical Chadband, and Mrs. Snagsby—who attempt to blackmail Sir Leicester about his wife's past and to withhold the vital missing will in the case of Jarndyce versus Jarndyce.

Bucket's first appearance, during the scene when Mr. Snagsby is summoned to Tulkinghorn's office to aid in the search for Jo, introduces the salient points of his character with remarkable economy:

> Mr. Snagsby is dismayed to see, standing with an attentive face between himself and the lawyer, at a little distance from the table, a person with a hat and stick in his hand, who was not there when he himself came in, and has not since entered by the door or by either of the windows. There is a press in the room, but its hinges have not creaked, nor has a step been audible upon the floor. Yet this third person stands there, with his attentive face, and his hat and stick in his hands, and his hands behind him, a composed and quiet listener. He is a stoutly built, steady-looking, sharp-eyed man in black, of about the middle-age. Except that he looks at Mr. Snagsby as if he were going to take his portrait, there is nothing very remarkable about him at first sight but his ghostly manner of appearing. (22.305–306)

The last sentence of this passage, in which the statement that "there is nothing very remarkable" about Inspector Bucket is qualified in both preceding and succeeding clauses, highlights his apparently contradictory nature. For even "at first sight" it is clear that the detective is simultaneously a very ordinary and a very extraordinary figure.

Like the policemen in the *Household Words* articles, Bucket is the incarnation of lower middle-class respectability: he is "stoutly built, steady-looking," and dressed in the sober black of the minor bureaucratic functionary. In subsequent scenes the details that define his social status are noted with care and relish. Dickens draws further attention to Bucket's dress—the brooch "composed of not much diamond and a good deal of setting" (22.308) which he wears in his shirt—and offers several glimpses of his comfortable but unpretentious private life: "Refreshed by sleep, Mr. Bucket rises betimes in the morning, and prepares for a field-day. Smartened up by the aid of a clean shirt and a wet hairbrush, with which instrument, on occasions of ceremony, he lubricates such thin locks as remain to him after his life of severe study, Mr. Bucket lays in a breakfast of two mutton chops as a foundation to work upon, together with tea, eggs, toast, and marmalade, on a corresponding scale" (54.720).

As in the earlier journalism, the detective's speech mannerisms are caught with particular success. Bucket speaks a language that combines unimpeachable respectability with a vitality lacking in more genteel dialects. It can display a vigorous humor reminiscent of Sam Weller: "You don't happen to know why they killed the pig, do you?" he asks Grandfather Smallweed, and answers himself, "Why they killed him . . . on account of his having so much cheek" (54.726). At other times his speech modulates into a tone of homely ease—he "likes a toothful of your fine old brown East Inder sherry better than anything you can offer him" (53.712)—or assumes a note of homely sententiousness—"Mrs. Bucket is as fond of children as myself, and as wishful to have 'em; but no. So it is. Worldly goods are divided unequally, and man must not repine" (49.670). These reminders of Bucket's solidly bourgeois status offer implicit reassurance to the reader: can a man who belongs so entirely to the world of Kensal Green be anything but the embodiment of rough though genial virtue?

Although Bucket appears as comfortingly familiar as the common household article after which he is named, he also exudes an aura of mysterious power which at times hints at the supernatural. In the passage that introduces him his apparently magical means of entering Mr. Tulkinghorn's room is stressed. Later, when Bucket is investigating Tulkinghorn's murder, the narrator comments: "Time and place cannot bind Mr. Bucket. Like man in the abstract, he is here to-day and gone to-morrow—but, very unlike man indeed, he is here again the next day. This evening he will be casually looking into the iron extinguishers at the door of Sir Leicester Dedlock's house in town; and to-morrow morning he will be walking on the leads at Chesney Wold, where erst the old man walked whose ghost is propitiated with a hundred guineas" (53.709).

This seemingly supernatural mobility is related to the easy nonchalance with which Bucket moves between the disparate milieus and social groups in the novel. Shortly after his first appearance he whisks the bewildered but impressed Mr. Snagsby from the sedate calm of Tulkinghorn's office to the slums of Tom-All-Alone's in search of Jo. Later, when seeking the lawyer's murderer, he shows a similar "adaptability to all grades" (53.717) of society, alternating between the below- and above-stairs worlds of the Dedlock household. This skill differentiates Bucket from the rest of the characters in the book, for they customarily remain trapped within their own isolated circle, unable or unwilling to make contact with the other groups of which society is composed.

In the opening scene with Mr. Snagsby a second and related aspect of Bucket's power appears: he is remarkable not only for his "ghostly manner of appearing" but also for his sharp eyes, his "attentive face," and his habit of looking at the law stationer "as if he were going to take his portrait." The suggestion of uncanny insight into other people's characters is quickly substantiated: when Mr. Snagsby shows himself to be momentarily at a loss, Bucket "dips down into the bottom of his mind" (22.306).

The result is a control over others similar to his control over the spatial environment: he can manipulate them like pieces on a chessboard. In conversation his personality is subtly adjusted to suit that of his interlocutor. Talking to Mr. Snagsby, he mentions a no doubt mythical uncle in the law stationery business; dining with the musical Bagnets, friends of Mr. George, he confesses that "when I was a boy I played the fife myself" (49.671–672) and proceeds to entertain them with a sentimental song. His entrance into the Dedlocks' parlor is something of a tour de force: "Mr. Bucket makes three distinctly different bows to these three people. A bow of homage to Sir Leicester, a bow of gallantry to Volumnia, and a bow of recognition to the debilitated cousin" (53.713).

The suggestion of flattery here is hardly accidental, for if Bucket adapts his own personality to suit the company, he also molds the company to suit himself. In conversation, he customarily creates whatever image of the other person is most likely to make them subservient to his own ends:

> "Yes! and lookee here, Mr. Snagsby," resumes Bucket, taking him aside by the arm, tapping him familiarly on the breast, and speaking in a confidential tone. "You're a man of the world, you know, and a man of business, and a man of sense. That's what *you are* . . . Now, it an't necessary to say to a man like you, engaged in your business, which is a business of trust and requires a person to be wide awake and have his senses about him, and his head screwed on tight . . . it an't necessary to say to a man like you, that it's best and wisest to keep little matters like this quiet. Don't you see? Quiet!" (22.306–307)

Here, the application of the technique to the law stationer is especially artful. The appeal to his business sense panders to his pride, while the implicitly menacing tone in which it is delivered arouses his constitutional cowardice. This aspect of Bucket's power extends even to relations with his social superiors. He begins his revelation of Lady Dedlock's secret by telling Sir Leicester: "you are a gentleman; and I know what a gentleman is, and what a gentleman is capable of. A gentleman can bear a shock, when it must come, boldly and steadily. A gentleman can make up his mind to stand up against almost any blow" (54.721). When Bucket is finished, the haughty peer is completely under his control, "relying on that officer alone of all mankind" (54.730).

Predictably, the other characters in the book are impressed but mystified by Inspector Bucket. He himself is given to a habit of self-identification: he tells people on meeting them, "I am Inspector Bucket of the Detective, I am" (e.g. 54.725). But the *mot de caractère* merely accentuates the problem. "Now you know me don't you" (57.780), he twice inquires of Esther during their search for Lady Dedlock. "What could I say but yes!" (57.580), she comments, as if she had been forced to commit herself only out of social politeness.

Mr. George, whose contact with the detective is extensive, can only venture that he is a "rum customer" (47.636). Several other characters resort to paradox in attempting to describe him. To Volumnia Dedlock he is "charmingly horrible" (53.717), while to Mademoiselle Hortense he is "angel and devil by turns" (54.738). Upon this last provocation Bucket responds enigmatically: "But I am in my regular employment, you must consider" (54.738). Moreover, when other characters arrive at a firm judgment, they contradict both themselves and each other. Mr. Bagnet is first completely charmed by Bucket and then equally sure he is a fraud. Simultaneously, in Sir Leicester Dedlock's estimation the detective has become transformed from a species of useful upper servant into the last trustworthy figure in a perplexing world.

It is to the quality of inconsistency, if not paradox, that the reader reverts in his own estimate of Bucket, for the policeman's actions show him to be both good and bad. The two other types of detection offered—Esther's desire to combine understanding with compassion and Tulkinghorn's destructive inquisitiveness—are juxtaposed in a single character. Although some of this ambivalence persists throughout the presentation of Bucket, a broad developmental pattern may be discerned: in his early appearances his detection tends to be harmful, while near the end of the book it becomes useful.[24] This change is accompanied by a significant structural shift: Bucket first appears in Tulkinghorn's office, but later, in the climactic pursuit of Lady Dedlock, he becomes the companion and guide of Esther.

From the start a number of motifs associate Bucket with

Tulkinghorn, the embodiment of bad detection. Both men, for example, wear black—a characteristic they share with most of the book's representatives of law and authority. Tulkinghorn himself possesses the power of apparently supernatural mobility. His "manner of coming and going between the two places [Lincoln's Inn and Chesney Wold], is one of his impenetrabilities" (42.582), and on one occasion he uses it in a way that directly echoes Bucket's appearance before the surprised Mr. Snagsby: "Mr. Guppy starts at seeing Mr. Tulkinghorn standing in the darkness opposite, with his hands behind him" (39.558).

These associative images have a firm counterpart in the workings of the plot, for Bucket's early role identifies him with Tulkinghorn's activities. Members of the Detective Department were, like the Runners whom they replaced, available for private hire. Dickens does not mention the fact in his journalism, preferring to see the force as "calmly and steadily engaged in the service of the public" (149) rather than as serving the interests of any particular group. But when Bucket first appears, he is in Tulkinghorn's pay and functions as an extension of the lawyer. On Tulkinghorn's behalf, for example, he has arrested Gridley, that emblematic victim of the Court of Chancery, "over and over again, for contempt" (24.350). As if to emphasize the point, Bucket arrives to serve a final warrant when Gridley is dying after his lifetime of suffering at the hands of lawyers and authorities.

Bucket's persecution of Jo, that other victim of society who dies in Mr. George's shooting gallery, is an extended and elaborate version of his treatment of Gridley. Here Bucket's villainy is illustrated with greater force, for the manner in which people treat Jo is commonly used as a touchstone to their true characters. Before Bucket's appearance the constable on the beat who tries to make Jo "move on" is used as a symbol of society's indifference toward the weak and helpless:

> Do you hear, Jo? It is nothing to you or to any one else, that the great lights of the parliamentary sky have failed for some few years, in this business, to set you the example of moving on. The one grand recipe remains for you—the profound philosophical prescription—the be-all and the end-all of your strange existence upon earth.

Move on! You are by no means to move off, Jo, for the great lights can't at all agree about that. Move on! (19.264)

The link between the preventive and the detective police is obvious, emphasized by both Bucket and Jo in their different ways. In Tulkinghorn's office Bucket tells the lawyer that "our people have moved this boy on" (22.306), and when Bucket discovers Jo in Tom-All-Alone's, the boy's first frightened re-action is "to think that he has offended against the law in not moving on far enough" (22.312). Bucket's subsequent pursuit of Joe is in itself the final enactment of the authorities' only solution: Jo is moved on to his grave.

The policeman on the beat is at least enforcing a theory of public order, however vague or mistaken. Bucket's persecu-tion of Jo lacks even this slender justification, for it is merely a piece of private dirty work. Tulkinghorn's curiosity about Lady Dedlock makes the crossing-sweeper an important wit-ness; and so Bucket must find him, use him and then move him on so he cannot reveal his evidence to anyone else. Like the lawyer's treatment of Lady Dedlock, the incident is simple exploitation In fact, in each case the victim comes to view the persecutor in a similar way. To Lady Dedlock the lawyer seems: "Always at hand. Haunting every place. No relief or security from him for a moment" (48.650). To Jo the detective seems an equally sinister and pervasive presence: "Very ap-prehensive of being overheard, Jo looks about him, and even glances up some ten feet at the top of a hoarding, and through the cracks in it, lest the object of his distrust should be looking over, or hidden on the other side" (46.630). "He's in all man-ner of places, all at wanst" (46.631), he explains to Woodcourt, the doctor who befriends him.

Although Bucket's actions are as harmful in their effects as Tulkinghorn's, his motives are different. The lawyer is driven by an obsessive desire for personal power, but Bucket is merely doing a job or, as he himself sees it, carrying out his duty. Moreover, his character is not wholly circumscribed by his work. Near the beginning of the novel Harold Skimpole, Jarndyce's parasitical friend, assures Coavinses, the "follerer" who comes to arrest him for debt, "We can separate you from your office; we can separate the individual from the pursuit"

(6.75). In Coavinses' case the distinction is irrelevant, for like most of the characters associated with the law, he is an extreme embodiment of the professional man. He is totally absorbed in his work and given to viewing the world from a standpoint that excludes all human concern. In Bucket, however, the man and the work are not merely separable but apparently at times in opposition.[25]

As he performs cruel tasks, Bucket exudes an air of kindly concern for his victims. The habit reaches something of a climax with the arrest of Mr. George, when he insists on using handcuffs but thoughtfully provides a cloak to conceal them from the curious gaze of passers-by. The conflict in Bucket's interests is emphasized by the chapter title, "Dutiful Friendship." Earlier, when serving the warrant on the dying Gridley, Bucket arrives suggestively disguised as a physician, a healer rather than a causer of suffering. At the deathbed he "good-naturedly offered such consolation as he could administer" (24.350). He exhorts Gridley to live to fight again another day: "Come, come!" he said from his corner. "Don't go on in that way, Mr. Gridley. You are only a little low. We are all of us a little low, sometimes. *I* am. Hold up, hold up! You'll lose your temper with the whole round of 'em again and again; and I shall take you on a score of warrants yet, if I have luck" (24.350). At one point Bucket even offers to exchange their roles of oppressor and oppressed: "He's welcome to drop into me, right and left, if he likes. I shall never take advantage of it" (24.351). Similarly, while helping to move Jo on to his grave, he also tries to put him in hospital and twice gives him money.

Such small acts of kindness, however, do not mitigate the effect of Bucket's actions. Jo and Gridley still die, and the innocent Mr. George still goes to prison. Moreover, the kindness is limited in itself: Dickens elsewhere mocks Mr. Snagsby's belief in the "magic balsam" (47.643) of the half-crown gift or the kindly word to the poor. Although Bucket's disguise as a doctor and his attempts to show compassion toward the inhabitants of Tom-All-Alone's invite the reader to compare him with Woodcourt, the comparison is to the policeman's disadvantage. As the narrator explains, Woodcourt has the gift of "avoiding patronage or condescension, or childishness" (46.626) in his dealings with the poor. Bucket, on the contrary, frequently mixes his kindness with a vein of pompous moralizing that reveals a fundamental failure to comprehend their plight. During his visit with Mr. Snagsby to Tom-All-Alone's he lectures the brickmaker's wife about her child: "you train him respectable, and he'll be a comfort to you, and look after you in your old age, you know" (22.311). Giving money to Jo, he remarks with similar inappositeness: "Take care how you spend it, and don't get yourself into trouble" (22.314).[26]

Yet these touches of compassion prevent Bucket's seeming entirely unsympathetic and so prepare the reader for the role the detective later plays in the book. Most simply, Bucket becomes a more important figure than before. Where he had earlier appeared only briefly and intermittently, he plays a vital part in the denouement of several of the mystery plots: arresting Hortense for Tulkinghorn's murder, revealing the truth about Lady Dedlock's past to her husband, dealing with the attempt by Smallweed and his associates to blackmail Sir Leicester, searching for Lady Dedlock after her flight from home, and finally, forcing Smallweed to hand over to Jarndyce the missing will in the Chancery suit. From these scenes he emerges as a benevolent force, his desire to do good no longer at odds with the nature of his work. His arrest of Hortense, for example, shows that law and authority can perform more useful tasks than harrying crossing-sweepers or serving writs on Chancery suitors. His search for Lady Dedlock is an errand of mercy. Taken together, his actions show that the detective can play an important role as the bringer of truth and clarity to a society crippled by mystery and confusion.

The importance of this role is emphasized by the narrative method adopted for the description of Tulkinghorn's murder and its aftermath. Once the groundwork has been laid at the beginning of the novel, the reader usually shares the narrator's omniscient view of events rather than the ignorance and perplexity of most of the characters: he is able to understand the significance of events as they happen. He is aware of the relationship between Esther and Lady Dedlock before they are themselves, and can follow the steps of Tulkinghorn's investigations with a comprehension which contrasts sharply with the bewilderment of Jo and Mr. Snagsby.

For the narration of Tulkinghorn's murder, however, Dickens uses a technique like that of the modern detective story. Vital facts are withheld, and attempts are made to mislead and confuse the reader. The crime itself is described only obliquely—"What's that? Who fired a gun or pistol? Where was it?" (48.660)—and suspicion is deliberately directed toward Lady Dedlock. Nor does the reader know of the real direction of Bucket's investigations until the scene in which Mademoiselle Hortense is accused. Only then does he learn that Bucket was never fully convinced of Mr. George's guilt, and that the detective and his wife have arranged an elaborate surveillance of the real criminal. The effect is not merely to create that sense of suspense and anticipation commonly associated with detective fiction but also to change the nature of both the reader's view of Bucket and his involvement in the narrative. For the first time the reader experiences the chaos and confusion of the world of *Bleak House* from the inside, without the presence of a reliable third-person narrator to guide and reassure him. Like the characters themselves, he can understand events only partially and make mistaken guesses at their true nature. In these circumstances he relies on Bucket, as he had earlier relied on the third-person narrator, to re-establish the clarity of vision which the shift in narrative method has temporarily destroyed.

In fact, the investigation of Tulkinghorn's death and the arrest of Hortense provide the book's most extended demonstration of Bucket's powers. During the progress of his inquiries he "walks in an atmosphere of mysterious greatness" (53.711); his finger becomes his "familiar demon" (53.709) and his notebook a "book of Fate" (53.712). Preparing to confront the murderess with evidence of her guilt, the detective is "composed, sure, confident" (54.720). He boasts to Sir Leicester Dedlock, "I don't suppose there's a move on the board that would surprise *me*" (54.722).

Yet Bucket's triumph is not entirely unalloyed. After her arrest Mademoiselle Hortense subjects him to a brief but telling catechism:

"Listen then, my angel," says she, after several sarcastic nods. "You are very spiritual. But can you restore him [Tulkinghorn] back to life?"

Mr. Bucket answers "Not exactly."

"That is droll. Listen yet one time. You are very spiritual. Can you make an honourable lady of Her?"

"Don't be so malicious," says Mr. Bucket.

"Or a haughty gentleman of *Him?*" cries Mademoiselle, referring to Sir Leicester with ineffable disdain. "Eh! O then regard him! The poor infant! Ha! ha! ha!"

"Come, come, why this is worse Parlaying than the other," says Mr. Bucket. "Come along!"

"You cannot do these things? Then you can do as you please with me. It is but the death." (54.739)

The fact that Bucket's powers are limited is emphasized at several points during the final part of the book. He blusters impressively in the face of the attempt to blackmail Sir Leicester about the secret of his wife's past, but he finally advises the peer to pay up. His production of the missing will promises a happy solution to Jarndyce versus Jarndyce, but is in fact proved irrelevant by the course of events. The case is forced to end because the Jarndyce estate has been absorbed in legal costs.

Although he may at times appear superhuman to the other characters, Bucket is ultimately neither magician nor demigod but merely an intelligent human. Despite his ability to interpret events that would otherwise remain confused and obscure, he can only partially affect their course. He cannot undo the past by bringing Tulkinghorn back to life, nor can he entirely control the present. The ending of Jarndyce versus Jarndyce is the culmination of an inevitable and destined pattern which is beyond the control of the human actors in the drama.

It is in the pursuit of the missing Lady Dedlock that this balance between success and failure in Bucket's work is most extensively demonstrated. On the one hand, he cannot alter the outcome of Lady Dedlock's tragic destiny; yet on the other, the combination of compassion and intelligence which he brings to the issue can affect the meaning it has for the other characters, particularly Esther.[27]

Throughout the pursuit Bucket's demeanor emphasizes the

fact that, at this point, he is a positive and benevolent figure. Tulkinghorn's inquiries into Lady Dedlock's past were associated with images of dust, rust, and decay, and the lawyer himself was shown in rigidly self-contained, static poses. Bucket, by contrast, is here associated with images of warmth and movement, and exudes an air of outgoing vitality:

> All this time, kept fresh by a certain enjoyment of the work in which he was engaged, he was up and down at every house we came to; addressing people whom he had never beheld before, as old acquaintances; running in to warm himself at every fire he saw; talking and drinking and shaking hands at every bar and tap; friendly with every waggoner, wheelwright, blacksmith, and toll-taker; yet never seeming to lose time, and always mounting to the box again with his watchful steady face, and his business-like "Get on, my lad!" (57.776)

Bucket's energy is not simply that of the bloodhound on the scent but is closely related to the compassionate and reassuring attitude he adopts toward Esther, his companion throughout the journey: "He was really very kind and gentle; and as he stood before the fire warming his boots, and rubbing his face with his forefinger, I felt a confidence in his sagacity which re-assured me" (57.766).

His role is further defined by the implicit parallels between the pursuit and two earlier scenes in the novel. Previously, he had sought Jo through the slums, taking Mr. Snagsby with him as a proof of good intentions. Here, again on the track of a missing person, he chooses his companion for the same reason. He explains to Jarndyce, "But if I follow her in company with a young lady, answering to the description of a young lady that she has a tenderness for—I ask no question, and I say no more than that—she will give me credit for being friendly" (56.762). In the first episode Bucket's purpose had been anything but friendly and he had conformed to one of the most familiar Dickensian stereotypes, the powerful villain pursuing the helpless waif. Now, the search is an errand of mercy: Bucket is charged to deliver Sir Leicester's generous message of forgiveness to his wife. In his relationship with Esther he becomes the protector and guardian of the waif. The point is emphasized by the manner in which their ride together recalls

Esther's first meeting with Jarndyce on her way to the school at Reading.

Yet clearly Bucket is different from either Jarndyce or the benevolent father-figure who appears so often in Dickens' fiction. He is, by his own declaration, a "practical" man (57.771); the wisdom which he represents is in every sense worldly. Whereas Jarndyce had been inclined to accept Harold Skimpole's childishness at face value, Bucket expresses a shrewder, more knowing opinion: "Whenever a person says to you that they are as innocent as can be in all concerning money, look well after your own money, for they are dead certain to collar it, if they can. Whenever a person proclaims to you 'In worldly matters I'm a child,' you consider that that person is only a-crying from being held accountable, and that you have got that person's number, and it's Number One" (57.771). This definitive judgment on Skimpole comes as a revelation to Esther, who had previously largely concurred in Jarndyce's more trusting and naive view. It thus epitomizes Bucket's role throughout the journey. Although he fails in the literal task in hand, that of saving Lady Dedlock, he performs another, equally important function: taking Esther out into the world and helping her to face its harsh realities. He becomes her guide, metaphorically as well as literally, in a crucial passage from innocence to experience.

The process is emphasized by the symbolic overtones with which their journey is surrounded. Bucket wakes Esther up in the middle of the night and takes her out of the comfort and security of Jarndyce's house into an alien, bewildering world: "I was far from sure that I was not in a dream. We rattled with great rapidity through such a labyrinth of streets, that I soon lost all idea of where we were" (57.766). The landscape through which they travel is full of sinister portents of the scene that awaits them at the end: "The river had a fearful look, so overcast and secret, creeping away so fast between the low flat lines of shore: so heavy with indistinct and awful shapes, both of substance and shadow: so death-like and mysterious" (57.767). The scene to which the detective finally guides Esther is a representation, in emblematic form, of the truth from which she has shrunk for much of the book: the spectacle of her mother, Lady Dedlock, reaching through the barred gateway of the burial ground toward the grave of her lover, Captain Hawdon. The mysterious family connections, so long obscured and rendered so destructive by their obscurity, are at last brought into the open and fully acknowledged.

For Esther the experience is painful. Yet the scene also hints at a regenerative process. For Esther it holds a promise expressed in the title of a subsequent chapter, "Beginning the World." The arrival of Esther and her guide occurs, the narrative is careful to note, at a moment of transition in the natural world when the snow is melting and the night giving way to morning. Once the truth is discovered and faced, the restrictive and shadowy influence of the past on the present begins to yield. Inspector Bucket has been unable to avert the inevitable end of a tragic process; but, with tact and sensitivity, he has helped the survivors to an understanding of the tragedy's significance.

5
Wilkie Collins
and Other Sensation Novelists

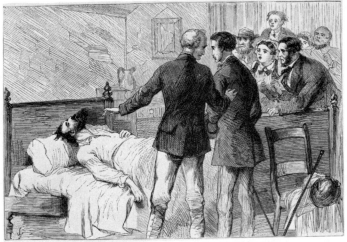

Dickens was the first major publicist for the police detective. In his journalism he seized on the Detective Department as on a personal discovery and treated it with a mixture of boyish awe and proprietary affection. In *Bleak House* he produced a memorable portrait of the new breed of police officer, showing how he might usefully be deployed amid the familiar plot motifs of the Victorian novel.

Dickens' achievement was frequently copied. When James Payn, himself an ex-member of the *Household Words* staff, introduced a portrait of Townshend, the Bow Street Runner, in his *Lost Sir Massingberd* (1864), his intention was apparently to defend the old detective system against the new: "In those early days, when the telegraph could not overtake the murderer speeding for his life, and set Justice upon her guard five hundred miles away, to intercept him, and when the sun was not the slave of the Law, to photograph the features of the doomed criminal, so that he can be recognized as easily as Cain, thief-catching was a much more protracted business than it is now; nevertheless, it was at least as certain." Yet once Townshend is established at the scene of the mystery, Payn's attempt at sketching a historical portrait of "the father of all the Fields and Pollakies of the present day" is defeated by memories of Dickens' creation.[1] The Runner has a habit of tapping his wineglass with his forefinger, refers to the title character as "Sir Massingberd Heath, baronet," and talks in an idiom infinitely more reminiscent of Bucket than of the refinements of Regency speech: "Now, the first thing as has to be done, gentlemen all—by which no offence is meant to the young lady—is this."[2]

In succeeding fiction echoes of "the immortal Bucket," as John Forster dubbed him, proved as long-lived as they were detailed.[3] Hawley Smart's *At Fault*, published some thirty years after *Bleak House* in 1883, introduces a clear inheritor of some of Bucket's magical and mysterious characteristics. Sergeant Usher, whose "very name caused terror to the tip-top professors of the art of burglary," has "a way of appearing at people's sides in a stealthy, ghost-like fashion positively appalling." He does not inspect the scene of the crime but "simply pervaded the town," and he records his discoveries in a notebook "which might almost have been called 'his familiar.' It was the black poodle of Faust."[4]

Although the minor writers of the age at times appear excessive in their imitation of Dickens, the strong familial resemblance that succeeding police detectives bear to Inspector Bucket, and to each other, cannot be ascribed solely to Dickens' influence. The rudiments of a literary stereotype were beginning to emerge before publication of either the *Household Words* articles or *Bleak House,* and Dickens' contribution to its development was for him a characteristic one. Always alert to popular tastes and concerned that his work should bear "the impress of the moving age," he merely gave this popular subject articulate expression and wider currency.[5] Inspector Bucket, though influential, is thus in no sense the "father" of succeeding fictional detectives. He is the most memorable and intelligent expression of a broadly based popular figure.

With the exception of Wilkie Collins the sensation novelists add little to Dickens' achievement. But taken as a whole, their work establishes the police detective as one of the most familiar literary stereotypes of the age, a figure as heavily conventionalized and as recurrent as the jolly tar of the melodrama or the innocent heroine of the fiction. By the time that Jules Verne came to write *Around the World in Eighty Days* (1873), the police detective had come to seem, in French eyes at least, as typical a feature of the English way of life as the phlegmatic and reserved gentleman. An ironic but good-humored portrait of Detective Fix, the man from Scotland Yard, takes its place in Verne's work beside the account of Phileas Fogg's eccentric traveling.

Physically, the typical fictional detective is clean-shaven (so that he can conveniently assume facial disguises), impassive, and keen-eyed, suggestive of continual shrewd observation. Otherwise his appearance may be that of a resoundingly lower middle-class and mildly comic bureaucrat, like Sergeant Delves in Mrs. Henry Wood's *Mrs. Halliburton's Troubles* (1862): "a portly man, with a padded breast, and a red face, who always looked as if he were throttling in his official costume."[6] More usually he is deliberately ordinary-looking, like Carter in Miss Braddon's *Henry Dunbar* (1864), whose "appearance was something between the aspect of a shabby-genteel half-pay captain and an unlucky stockbroker" and who has "no distinctive stamp upon him, however slight, that marked him as the hunter of a murderer."[7]

Like Bucket, succeeding police detectives commonly work on private hire or for a specific reward, but their attitude is that of the public servant rather than the paid hireling. Miss Braddon's Carter "knew that he did his duty, and that society could not hold together unless some such men as himself—clear-headed, brave, resolute, and unscrupulous in the performance of unpleasant work—were willing to act as watchdogs for the protection of the general fold, and to the terror of savage and marauding beasts."[8] They eschew the vices of the mercenary and the blood-money man. Their attitude to criminals, rather than being vindictive or bloodthirsty, is commonly as compassionate as their duty permits. Sergeant Usher in *At Fault,* though "keen for a conviction," "had no craving for any extreme sentence against the unfortunate he had brought face to face with the gallows." Police detectives treat the other actors in the drama with sympathy. Usher is "in cases like the present always anxious to spare the feelings of the unfortunate's relatives as much as might be."[9] In the cruder literature of the period the detective can be blatantly sentimental. Carter, in Tom Taylor's 1865 stage version of Miss Braddon's novel, explains his motives: "You see I'm rather sweet on the job. It ain't so much the reward, though two hundred pounds ain't to be sneezed at, nor the man [the victim] himself—he was a bad lot—but it's his daughter, as nice, pretty-looking, hard-working a girl as you'd wish to see, sir; she's set her heart on spotting the parties [the murderers]—finding on 'em out that is."[10]

The considerable respect and affection with which Victorian writers and their audience had come to regard police detectives by the 1860s is further illustrated by their customary role in the action of such novels. They tackle crime and mystery with a native shrewdness and an armory of police techniques rudimentary in modern eyes but then sufficiently novel to be regarded by contemporaries with an almost superstitious awe. For example, they can trace a missing man through the banknotes he was known to be carrying at the time of his disappearance, or use the telegraph system to transmit information about a wanted suspect.

This awe, however, has its limits. In *Bleak House* Dickens is careful to circumscribe the powers attributed to Bucket and to show the ways in which the detective could not completely control the action. This element of fallibility is echoed in the minor fiction, though in cruder ways. Police detectives are shown to be intelligent, and they always acquit themselves honorably in investigations, but they rarely succeed entirely. In *Mrs. Halliburton's Troubles,* for example, Sergeant Delves, after neatly disposing of a case of petty theft, fails to solve the murder mystery that occupies most of the final part of the book. He arrests the wrong man, who is acquitted by the local magistrates—a verdict that Delves accepts with philosophical resignation and good humor. Townshend in *Lost Sir Massingberd,* after expending considerable energy trying to trace the missing baronet of the title, finally departs from the scene of the action with the problem still unsolved. In *Henry Dunbar* Carter correctly identifies the murderer but fails to catch him. He is foiled in a lengthy chase sequence which clearly echoes Bucket's pursuit of Lady Dedlock: as in *Bleak House,* the fugitive dispatches in a different direction a disguised surrogate whom the detective mistakenly follows.

These instances of failure are to some extent explained by the authors' desire to retain a structural balance in their work. The detectives are not, after all, protagonists but are merely among the more interesting secondary characters, and their complete success might make them predominate unduly over the book's closing pages. As it is, their ultimate failure usually functions as a convenient device for removing them discreetly from the action, leaving the hero and heroine to occupy the center of interest at the end. There is also a deeper reason for this insistence on the detective's failure, a reason that partly explains the novelists' reluctance to make him more than an interesting supernumerary. It derives from the writers' almost obsessive reliance on the abstractions of Providence and Destiny to dictate the progress of their plots and to bring the action to neat and satisfactory conclusions in which mystery is dispelled, the good rewarded, and the bad punished.

The detectives themselves often express cynicism about

these abstract notions and show a confident belief in the capacity of humans to order things satisfactorily without external aids. Townshend brusquely declares: "Well, sir . . . you see judgements isn't much in my way. When I catches a chap he generally knows it's judgement and execution too; but, barring that, I doubt whether there's much of a special Providence for rascals—even when they rob a Church minister." [11] Carter, in Tom Taylor's version of *Henry Dunbar*, remarks in a more philosophical vein, "The old saying is 'murder will out,' but how would it be without a branch of the force, the metropolitan I mean, to start it?" [12]

The novelists, however, thought differently. Their plotting insists on the presence of a guiding hand of Providence which works through apparent coincidence to solve the baffling mystery and to cause the criminal to betray himself by confession or to destroy himself by accident. At the end of *Mrs. Halliburton's Troubles* the solution to the Dare murder mystery emerges when the hero fortuitously encounters the real murderer, who, being on the point of death, obligingly confesses. Anticipating the reader's query as to what would have happened if the two had not thus met, Mrs. Wood primly remarks, "It was not chance that led them." [13] In a similar vein, Joseph Wilmot, the murderer who eludes Carter's clutches at the end of *Henry Dunbar*, is conveniently drowned in a storm at sea.

The belief in a Providence which discreetly orders the affairs of men can be the expression of a sophisticated religious philosophy, and the idea that "murder will out" can draw considerable support from theories of criminal psychology. Dickens, indeed, was aware of both of these notions, and in his novels the familiar plot paraphernalia with which they are associated take on a valid symbolic significance. The order which finally emerges is, in Edmund Wilson's words, "a revelatory symbol of something that the author wanted seriously to say." [14] But in the minor fiction of period such conviction is lacking, and Providence and Destiny are unmistakably terms which have come adrift from their intellectual moorings. The bland manner in which they are bandied about, and the neatness and intricacy of the plot machinery for which they serve as an excuse, merely accentuate the sense of an underlying intellectual void. [15]

Today *The Moonstone*, published in 1868, is probably the best remembered and most widely read of Wilkie Collins' works. In large part this is owing to its commonly accepted status as the first English detective novel. In histories of the genre it is customarily treated as the one really significant mid-Victorian contribution to a form whose development otherwise lay in the hands of Poe, Emile Gaboriau, and Arthur Conan Doyle. Abandoning the multiple plotting dear to the Victorian novelist's heart, Collins concentrates the action of the book on a single mysterious event, theft of the exotic diamond of the title from Rachel Verinder, the full truth of which is carefully concealed until the end. In *The Moonstone* the reader encounters for the first time in English fiction that world, now so familiar in modern detective novels, where all the apparently incidental details of the narrative are made to contribute to the final elucidation of the problem.

Throughout *The Moonstone* mystery arises from people's difficulty in viewing each other correctly.[16] Collins' preoccupation with such problems is implied by the book's narrative method, a succession of eyewitness reports. The effect is to provide a continually shifting viewpoint on the action, offering not merely different but sometimes contradictory views of the same event or character. Thus, the professional philanthropist Godfrey Ablewhite appears to Gabriel Betteredge, the Verinder family retainer and one of the story's main narrators, to be merely a skillful histrionic performer with a handkerchief and a glass of water. Yet to Miss Clack, the Evangelical spinster who takes over the narrative from Betteredge, Ablewhite is a living embodiment of the Christian hero.

These problems of perception begin in the Prologue and are introduced by the Moonstone itself. The anonymous narrator who describes Colonel Herncastle's theft of the stone from the Indian temple is faced by what is essentially a problem of circumstantial evidence. He cannot be sure whether Herncastle added murder to theft by killing the guardians of the diamond. Circumstances strongly suggest that Herncastle is a murderer, but "I have no evidence but moral evidence bring forward" (Prologue 16).[17] Though sufficiently convinced of the strength of his "moral evidence" to refuse to associate with Herncastle, the narrator is finally obliged to submit the problem to the individual judgment of his readers, the other members of his family: "Let our relatives, on either side, form their own opinions on what I have written, and decided for themselves whether the aversion I now feel towards this man is well or ill founded" (Prologue 16).

Colonel Herncastle's bequest of the Moonstone to his relative, the young Rachel Verinder, poses the same problem in a more extreme form. The available information permits of two entirely different explanations of the motive behind the Colonel's gift. Franklin Blake, the novel's hero, ponders: "In bringing the Moonstone to my aunt's house, am I serving his vengeance blindfold, or am I vindicating him in the character of a penitent and Christian man?" (Betteredge 6.55).

Shortly after Franklin brings it to the country house where Rachel lives with Lady Verinder, the Moonstone is stolen; it disappears during the night from Rachel's bedroom. Confusions multiply, creating a network of mutual misunderstanding, suspicion, and doubt. Rosanna Spearman, a servant in the house, concludes that Franklin is the thief. She is misled by her own wishes and expectations: "I had believed you to be guilty . . . more because I wanted you to be guilty than for any other reason" (Blake 4.342). Herself an ex-thief, Rosanna is secretly and hopelessly in love with Franklin; if he too is a thief, this will reduce him to her level and allow her to be of help by shielding him from suspicion and by using her criminal contacts to dispose of the stone. The effect of her suspicion on Rosanna is to create a pattern of behavior which makes her seem, in other eyes, to be a likely suspect herself.

Similarly Rachel, who believed that she saw Franklin take the stone from her bedroom cabinet, remembers the hints of profligacy about his character and proceeds to create a wholly mistaken image of him: a young man beset by creditors who has been driven to a particularly dishonorable form of crime. As in the case of Rosanna, her suspicions cause her to behave in ways that make her seem guilty herself. She is distraught and secretive, refuses to speak to the police, and hints cryptically that she knows the solution to the diamond's disappearance. Observing these signs, the detective Sergeant Cuff constructs an image of her character similar to that which she has constructed of Franklin Blake: a genteel young girl with dressmakers' bills that she dare not reveal to her relatives, forced to steal and sell a family heirloom. In all these cases the hypotheses reached are reasonable; yet all illustrate the limitations to which the individual's view of his fellows is subject. His judgment may be misled by superficial appearances, by his own expectations, or simply by an inadequate knowledge of the full pattern of events.

The end of the book provides a retrospective clarification of these mistakes. The suspicions that had separated Franklin and Rachel are dispelled; they are able to confess their love for each other and to provide an appropriate comedic resolution by their marriage. The villain Godfrey Ablewhite is identified and his true nature revealed. Sergeant Cuff reports:

> The side turned up to the public view presented the spectacle of a gentleman, possessed of considerable reputation as a speaker at charitable meetings, and endowed with administrative abilities, which he placed at the disposal of various Benevolent Societies, mostly of the female sort. The side kept hidden from the general notice exhibited this same gentleman in the totally different character of a man of pleasure, with a villa in the suburbs which was not taken in his own name, and with a lady in the villa who was not taken in his own name either. (Cuff 475)

Although the conclusion of the book presents an ordered picture in which people's true natures are brought to light and their misunderstandings of each other corrected, it does not entirely replace the earlier exploration of psychological complexity with a simple, one-dimensional view of human affairs. In the case of Franklin Blake the discovery of the truth involves the revelation of a form of double life altogether more perplexing than Godfrey Ablewhite's conventional suburban peccadilloes. The hero of the book, so anxious to solve the mystery and to establish his own innocence, is brought fact to face with a disturbing truth: "Thou art the man." Though Ablewhite was the real villain, Franklin was the original thief of the diamond, if only in a technical sense. On the night of the theft, he had unknowingly been given a dose of opium by the local doctor, Mr. Candy. Franklin had taken the diamond while in a somnambulistic trance and had entirely forgotten the incident on waking next morning.

In his portrait of Sergeant Cuff, the most important of the novel's several detectives, Collins was indebted to the example of Dickens' Inspector Bucket. Yet he was not overawed by his mentor, and his achievement does not suffer substantially by comparison. Cuff is one of his most felicitous creations. To T. S. Eliot he seemed "the perfect detective," preferred explicitly to Sherlock Holmes and implicitly to Inspector Bucket.[18]

Collins handles the stereotype of the police detective with skill and affectionate relish. Betteredge describes Cuff's arrival at the scene of the crime:

> A fly from the railway drove up as I reached the lodge; and out got a grizzled, elderly man, so miserably lean that he looked as if he had not got an ounce of flesh on his bones in any part of him. He was dressed all in decent black, with a white cravat round his neck. His face was as sharp as a hatchet, and the skin of it was as yellow and dry and withered as an autumn leaf. His eyes, of a steely light gray, had a very disconcerting trick, when they encountered your eyes, of looking as if they expected something more from you than you were aware of yourself. His walk was soft; his voice was melancholy; his long lanky fingers were hooked like claws. He might have been a parson, or an undertaker, or any thing else you like, except what he really was. (Betteredge 12.111)

The manner at once decently respectable and difficult to place, the unusually perceptive eyes, the hint of predatory power in the clawlike hands—all these are conventional motifs. In similar vein, Cuff's manner is imperturbable and impassive: "Sergeant Cuff never laughed. On the few occasions when any thing amused him, he curled up a little at the corners of the lips, nothing more" (Betteredge 14.130). He is sympathetic in his treatment of the other characters, but in his own mournful and laconic way: "Collar me again, Mr. Betteredge. If it's any vent to your feelings, collar me again" (Betteredge 16.154), he urges the house steward, in a scene reminiscent of Bucket encouraging Gridley to "drop into him." He makes oracular utterances pleasantly tantalizing to both the other characters and the reader:

> "Can you guess yet," inquired Mr. Franklin, "who has stolen the Diamond?"

"Nobody has stolen the Diamond," answered Sergeant Cuff.

We both started at that extraordinary view of the case, and both earnestly begged him to tell us what he meant.

"Wait a little," said the Sergeant. "The pieces of the puzzle are not all put together yet." (Betteredge 12.120)

What is most notable in Collins' achievement is the manner in which the conventional motifs of characterization are molded to the book's peculiar thematic preoccupations. Cuff is not merely mysterious in conventional ways. Entering a world in which mystery derives from the complexities of character and the difficulties that people experience in judging each other, he himself becomes the focus, as well as the book's main exemplification, of such problems.

As Betteredge notes, the detective's character contains an inherent contradiction: he is a thief-catcher whose main hobby is rose-growing. Questioned about his disparate interests, Cuff explains: "If you will look about you (which most people won't do) . . . you will see that the nature of a man's tastes is, most times, as opposite as possible to the nature of a man's business. Show me any two things more opposite one from the other than a rose and a thief, and I'll correct my tastes accordingly—if it isn't too late at my time of life" (Betteredge 12.113). Here the contradictoriness is part of that careful segmentation of life into work and private affairs which so fascinated Dickens, as in the portrait of Wemmick in *Great Expectations.* Moreover, Cuff's personality is capable of sudden and radical changes. After his retirement he returns to the action "as dreary and as lean as ever," but transformed from the epitome of the city dweller into an "innocent countryman": "He wore a broad-brimmed white hat, a light shooting-jacket, white trowsers, and drab gaiters. He carried a stout oak stick. His whole aim and object seemed to be to look as if he had lived in the country all his life. When I complimented him on his metamorphosis, he declined to take it as a joke. He complained, quite gravely, of the noises and the smells of London. I declare I am far from sure that he did not speak with a slightly rustic accent!" (Blake II, 1.459).

Complex himself, Cuff provokes widely differing and usually inaccurate reactions from other people. The scene in which he interviews the servants of the household about the theft provides a microcosm of his relations with other characters. The kaleidoscopic and contradictory portrait of him which emerges is due to both the subtle changes of his own personality and the particular prejudices of the various observers:

> I sent them in, one by one, as desired. The cook was the first to enter the Court of Justice, otherwise my room. She remained but a short time. Report, on coming out: "Sergeant Cuff is depressed in his spirits; but Sergeant Cuff is a perfect gentleman." My lady's own maid followed. Remained much longer. Report, coming out: "If Sergeant Cuff doesn't believe a respectable woman, he might keep his opinion to himself, at any rate!" Penelope went next. Remained only a moment or two. Report, on coming out: "Sergeant Cuff is much to be pitied. He must have been crossed in love, father, when he was a young man." The first house-maid followed Penelope. Remained, like my lady's maid, a long time. Report, on coming out: "I didn't enter her ladyship's service, Mr. Betteredge, to be doubted to my face by a low police officer!" Rosanna Spearman went next. Remained longer than any of them. No report on coming out—dead silence, and lips as pale as ashes. Samuel, the footman, followed Rosanna. Remained a minute or two. Report, on coming out: "Whoever blacks Sergeant Cuff's boots ought to be ashamed of himself." Nancy, the kitchen-maid, went last. Remained a minute or two. Report, on coming out: "Sergeant Cuff has a heart; *he* doesn't cut jokes, Mr. Betteredge, with a poor hard-working girl." (Betteredge 14.131)

Earlier Betteredge, who records these different impressions, had himself been betrayed into an equally misleading view of the detective on the basis of physical appearance. Whereas Seegrave, the blundering local man, seemed to him "the most comforting officer you could wish to see," Cuff, who brings tact and good sense to the mystery, appeared both disappointing and alarming: "a less comforting officer to look at for a family in distress, I defy you to discover, search where you may" (Betteredge 11.100, 12.111).

Reacting against his initial judgment, Betteredge accepts the common view of the detective as "the great Cuff" and "the celebrated Cuff." These phrases, picked up by Franklin Blake in his narrative, echo ironically through the book, for they represent as serious a misjudgment as was Betteredge's original impression. In the portrait of Cuff, the conventional fallibility of the police detective is stressed, and it constitutes a major theme of the book.

Collins' special interest in the policeman's fallibility is enforced by a comparison of the novel with the criminal case which he used as a partial source, the Constance Kent case of 1860.[19] Inspector Jonathan Whicher, one of the policemen whom Dickens had interviewed for his articles in *Household Words*, was called in to investigate the savage and apparently motiveless murder of Francis Kent, a four-year-old boy living in Road, a village bordering Somerset and Wiltshire. He arrested Constance Kent, the sixteen-year-old daughter of the family and stepsister of the dead child. Having deduced that one of Constance's nightgowns was missing, Whicher argued that it had become bloodstained during the killing and had subsequently been destroyed.

Whicher's action shocked contemporary observers, who preferred to believe that savage and senseless killings were done by tramps, servants, or foreigners rather than by adolescent girls of good family. At a preliminary hearing Whicher himself was described by the defense counsel as "a man eager in pursuit of the murderer, and anxious for the reward which has been offered," and the case against the girl was dismissed by the magistrates.[20] The detective returned to London in bad odor with both the general public and his superiors at Scotland Yard; shortly afterward he retired. In 1865 Constance Kent confessed to the murder in a statement whose details strikingly corroborated Whicher's deductions.

The Moonstone borrows several details from the case, most obviously the bungled local investigation and the business of Franklin Blake's missing nightgown.[21] But it makes one striking and central change: the final solution of the mystery affords no triumphant vindication of the policeman's deductions. Cuff tackles the problem with good sense and professional expertise; the hypothesis he puts forward, that Rachel herself is the thief, is plausible and well supported by the evidence. Yet after disappearing from the action for a time, he returns not to triumph in the accuracy of his original theories, but to admit that he was wrong. His intervention in the mystery serves merely to illustrate yet again the errors to which the individual's view of a complex series of events is subject.

The realization comes as a shock to those characters who insist on mythologizing him into "the great Cuff," but a knowledge of his own limitations is implicit in the detective's manner from the start. Where Bucket had been magnetic, energetic, and hard-working, Cuff exudes a melancholy, autumnal air, a "world-weary, half-bitter compassion."[22] His interest in roses is not, as it would have been with Bucket, an ingenious ploy designed to further his investigations but simply the genuine passion of a man already anticipating the pleasures of retirement. When, near the end of the book, the mystery is solved by others and his own failure is made completely clear, he accepts the news with the resignation of the hardened and mildly disillusioned professional:

> "There's only one thing to be said about the matter, on my side, I completely mistook my case. How any man living was to have seen things in their true light, in such a situation as mine was at the time, I don't profess to know. But that doesn't alter the facts as they stand. I own that I made a mess of it. Not the first mess, Mr. Blake, which has distinguished my professional career! It's only in books that the officers of the detective force are superior to the weakness of making a mistake." (Blake II, 1.459)

The effect of Cuff's removal from the action—he receives his *congé* from Lady Verinder about a third of the way through the book and makes only a brief reappearance at the end to have the honor of arresting Ablewhite—is thus profoundly dissimilar from, say, the absence of Sherlock Holmes during much of *The Hound of the Baskervilles*. It is not that a Godlike figure has disappeared from the stage, leaving both audience and actor groping in the dark, but simply that another human being, intelligent but no less fallible than most humans, has done his best and gone his way. After Cuff's departure his place is taken by a succession of amateur detectives—Bruff, Murthwaite, and Ezra Jennings—to whose investigations the antics of the prurient Miss Clack form a comic counterpoint.

Of these later detectives, Bruff and Murthwaite are negligible. Bruff is merely a routine presentation of a character familiar in Collins' fiction, having already appeared in *The Woman in White* in the person of Gilmore: the stolid, decent-minded family lawyer. Murthwaite, the traveler and expert on Oriental matters, has the correct physical equipment for a detective, since he is taciturn and has a "very steady attentive eye" (Betteredge 10.80), but his presence smacks of a structural contrivance. Collins needed to explain the role of the three Hindus in the action and wished to convince his readers of the factual basis for some of the more exotic Oriental touches in the book, so he decided to use Murthwaite as a mouthpiece.

The character of Ezra Jennings, by contrast, is of considerable interest. The doctor's assistant represents one of Collins' few successful experiments in a serious, rather than divertingly comic, study of eccentricity. As an amateur detective, Jennings is the fully developed counterpart to Cuff. Here, as in the portrait of the Sergeant, the detective forms the focus of the book's preoccupation with the complexities of character and character judgment. Jennings' physical appearance is a mass of contradictions: a combination of youthfulness and age, of a genteel manner with a complexion of "gypsy darkness" and a nose of "the fine shape and modeling so often found among the ancient people of the East" (Blake 4.343). Even his hair is piebald: "by some freak of Nature, [it] had lost its color in the most startlingly partial and capricious manner" (Blake 4.343). His life is a dislocated affair, for in the daytime he performs the humdrum duties of a doctor's assistant, while at night he inhabits a private world of opium fantasies. Moreover, he is continually the victim of prejudice: "his appearance is against him to begin with" (Blake 4.344), explains Gabriel Betteredge. Jennings later reveals to Franklin Blake that he has spent his life suffering under an unjust accusation of crime which he has been unable to rebut.

The hints of Orientalism about his appearance and his opium addiction suggest a mysterious communion with those elements of which the mystery is composed: the theft of an Indian diamond by a man in an opium trance. But Jenning's method is strictly rational. In fact, it embodies an approach to detection more solidly based on scientific rationalism than is

that of Cuff, who relied on elementary logic and police procedure, or of any preceding English fictional detective. When
Mr. Candy falls ill and lapses into delirium, Jennings is able to
detect in the doctor's wanderings a connected thread of
thought about the dose of opium given to Franklin Blake on
the night of the crime. This act of interpretation is a triumph
of scientific analysis which echoes Legrand's solution of the
cryptogram in Poe's story "The Gold Bug": "I have penetrated
through the obstacle of the disconnected expression to the
thought which was underlying it connectedly all the time"
(Blake 10.408). Faced with the problem of the missing diamond, Jennings forms a hypothesis based on his own knowledge of opium, buttresses it with quotations from scholarly
medical sources, and then subjects it to an elaborate empirical
test—that reconstruction of the crime which forms the dramatic climax of the book.

Ezra Jennings is not entirely responsible for the solution of
the mystery. The book's detectives act not in succession but as
a progressively expanding group out of whose combined activities the truth finally emerges. Each of them contributes
something to the solution, but none of them is wholly right.
Sergeant Cuff notices the smear on the freshly painted door of
Rachel's room and realizes that it will have left a distinguishing mark on the thief's clothing. Although the deduction
is correct, Cuff misidentifies the thief; he believes that the
diamond was stolen by Rosanna Spearman acting in conspiracy with Rachel. Murthwaite is able to explain the role of the
three Indians who follow in the tracks of the stolen diamond,
but contributes little else to the solution of the mystery. Bruff
helps to locate the diamond in the London bank, but doubts
Jennings' correct hypothesis that it had originally been taken
by Franklin Blake in an opium-induced trance. The work of
the book's detectives thus parallels its narrative method. The
discovery of the truth is a group affair, emerging from the successive reports of individual witnesses and observers.

Yet Collins' narrative is hardly a celebration of the powers of
collective reason. Although the group of detectives is finally
able to achieve a communal solution, the outcome is the result
of factors beyond the reach of reason—in fact, to those Victorian favorites Providence and Destiny. From the beginning

of the book the sequence of events surrounding the diamond is presented as the working-out of a destined pattern. The stone carries a curse with it, originating in the Hindu god's prediction of "certain disaster to the presumptuous mortal who laid hands on the sacred gem, and to all of his house and name who received it after him" (Prologue 13). Similarly, the activities of the book's detectives are indebted to a benign force of Providence, the counterpart to the evil destiny connected with the Moonstone. As is usual in Victorian fiction, this Providence manifests itself through an elaborate series of apparent coincidences.

The appearance of a supernumerary like Murthwaite, primed with arcane information about Hindu customs, seems suspiciously fortuitous, but the hand of Providence becomes even more blatantly obtrusive in the case of Jennings' intervention. Jennings makes his first appearance immediately after Franklin Blake, reading the letter from Rosanna Spearman which assumes him to be the thief, has cried out in despair:

> "Then, Betteredge—as far as I can see now—I am at the end of my resources. After Mr. Bruff and the Sergeant, I don't know of a living creature who can be of the slightest use to me."
> As the words passed my lips some person outside knocked at the door of the room. (Blake 4.343)

The implication that it is not really Ezra Jennings, but Providence in disguise, who knocks on the door so obligingly on cue is strengthened by further events. Despite his preoccupation with his own affairs, Franklin Blake finds that his brief meeting with Jennings has made a deep and "perfectly unaccountable" (Blake 5.345) impression on him. Subsequently, when Blake lays his problem before Jennings, the latter responds with a brief history of his own life, a refracted version of Blake's predicament, that of the innocent man suffering under suspicions which he is unable to dispel.

Collins' use of providential patterns to resolve the mystery reveals his limitations. In *The Moonstone* the ideas of Providence and Destiny rest on no firmer intellectual foundation than in, say, the work of Miss Braddon. The opportunities that they offer for the neat conclusion or the dramatic moment are merely employed by Collins with greater technical skill and panache. Although his initial insights into the sources of mystery put him on a level with Dickens, the means on which he relies to dispel the mystery link him immutably with the lesser writers of the age.

Between *The Moonstone* and the publication of Arthur Conan Doyle's *A Study in Scarlet* in 1887 there were no major contributions to the literature of detection. Dickens' *The Mystery of Edwin Drood* remains merely a tantalizing fragment, while Collins' own later experiments with detective literature bear unmistakable signs of that decline which marks all of his later work.[23] Otherwise the 1870s and 1880s were a period of minor talent and minor works. Yet the fiction of these years shows a significant, albeit ultimately inconclusive, change in the presentation of the detective. The respect and affection with which the policeman had been treated in the fiction of the middle years of the century diminishes, to be replaced by a growing vein of disillusionment and cynicism. The origins of this trend can be found in the history of the Detective Department.[24]

One of the chief factors that had won public confidence for the police during the mid-century was their freedom from the corruption which had bedeviled the older system of law enforcement. But in 1877 the force's reputation for honesty was rudely shaken by the Old Bailey trial of four inspectors from the Detective Department for their involvement, dating over a period of several years, in a fraudulent betting system run by two professional confidence tricksters. One of the policemen was acquitted, while the other three were sentenced to two years' hard labor.

As the trial of the detectives awakened memories of the days of the blood-money men, so a widely publicized case of 1880 raised another old but not entirely forgotten issue: the ethics of detection. The trial of a chemist named Titley for performing illegal abortions showed that the police, in their anxiety to gather evidence, had acted as *agents provocateurs*. The judge remarked uneasily that "there is a fluency and readiness of invention, and a facility of employing *spies* to go and lie, which is very painful to witness."[25] The Home Secretary conceded that "the cases in which it is necessary or justifiable for the police to resort to artifice of the description practised in this case must be rare indeed. As a rule, the police ought not to set traps for people." [26]

Such debacles are reflected in the fiction of the period. In *Checkmate* (1870–1871) Sheridan Le Fanu had already briefly introduced an ex-police detective, dismissed from the force for unspecified but sinister reasons, who has more in common with the old-style thief-taker than with Bucket or Cuff. Paul Davies is sleazy: "a tall thin fellow, shabbily dressed, standing nearly behind the door, with a long neck, and a flat mean face, slightly pitted with smallpox, rather pallid, who was smiling lazily, with half-closed eyes." His approach to his work is that of the trickster: "Paul Davies was, indeed, a man of that genius which requires to proceed by strategem, cherishing an abhorrence of straight lines, and a picturesque love of the curved and angular." [27] The last policeman to appear in Collins' work is also a corrupt and unsympathetic figure. The short story "Who Killed Zebedee?" which was originally published in 1881 and later included in the collection *Little Novels* (1887) under the title "Mr. Policeman and the Cook," is the dying confession of a man who, as a young and ambitious police detective, had concealed the solution of a murder case which he was assigned to investigate.

Although these literary echoes of actual incidents recall the older days of the thief-takers, the police force was by this time an established institution, deeply embedded in the English way of life and progressively assuming the proportions of a major governmental bureaucracy. The growth of the Detective Department itself was initially a slow business. Its staff, eight at its creation in the 1840s, had increased to only fifteen at the death of Sir Richard Mayne, the Commissioner, in 1868. However, under the supervision of the new Commissioner it grew to a membership of 260. In 1878 it was transformed into the Criminal Investigation Department—the name it still bears—under the direction of Howard Vincent, who had prepared for the task by making a survey of the workings of the Sûreté. Far more than a change of name was involved: its organization was restructured and during the next six years its size increased to nearly 800. "The Criminal Investigation Department," one police historian has commented, ". . . was in effect a new force. It was the first real attempt to put detection on a scientific footing."[28]

Such developments promised, and no doubt to a large extent provided, greater efficiency in the detection of crime. Yet unfortunately the police failed in some of the more famous cases of the age. The Fenians caused particular trouble. In 1867 they attacked Clerkenwell Prison, where two of their comrades were detained, despite the fact that the police had received advance warning of their plans. In the 1880s the Fenians included Scotland Yard itself among the many targets for their bomb attacks. A number of unsolved murders in the London area in 1872 and 1873 caused widespread anxiety. This, however, was merely a prelude to mass panic caused during the autumn of 1888 by the Jack the Ripper murders. Jack the Ripper induced something like a national hysteria, and the public, when it turned for comfort to the police, was greeted by a spectacle of bungling and inefficiency which at times verged on the farcical.

As early as 1868 the *Daily News* lamented: "Of late years the old confidence in the police has diminished. Whether as detectives or protectives, the public mistrusts them."[29] Anthony Trollope noted in *The Eustace Diamonds* (1871–1873) that press commentary on "the incompetence or slowness of the police" was "very common," although he hastened to add his opinion that "in nine cases out of ten it is unjust."[30] The *Daily Telegraph*, writing when the murders of 1872–1873 were causing concern, drew the sad conclusion: "The Inspector Buckets, of 'Bleak House,' the detective heroes of Mr. Wilkie Collins's novels have created an utterly false impression as to the capabilities of our police force."[31]

Later novelists, as well as Collins himself in his later fiction, were not slow to set the record right. For them, as for the general public, the police force had lost much of the novelty it had possessed when Dickens wrote his *Household Words* articles, and familiarity had bred contempt. The gradual transformation of police detectives from colorful figures like Field and Whicher, members of a small group, into functionaries of an impersonal bureaucracy made them less easy to dramatize or romanticize, while the policemen's failures made it increasingly tempting to satirize them. When Hawley Smart in *At Fault* (1883) shows Sergeant Usher brilliantly solving a mysterious crime, the tone is both defensive and belligerent. Usher soliloquizes, "I don't think the public will regard the police as duffers much longer when they've heard my exposition of the Bunbury mystery."[32]

Smart's attitude in an earlier novel, *False Cards* (1873), reflected current trends more directly when he named his police detective Bullock—a striking change from the earlier habit of giving policemen names, like Hawkshaw or Delves, suggestive of penetration and acumen. The typical police detective in the fiction of the seventies and eighties is a stolid and unimaginative bureaucrat, faithfully but mindlessly applying a simple set of official rules to the cases that come his way. A character in Collins' "My Lady's Money" (1877) remarks condescendingly: "No doubt they do their best, and take the greatest pains in following the routine to which they have been trained. It is their misfortune, not their fault, that there is no man of superior intelligence among them—I mean no man who is capable, in great emergencies, of placing himself above conventional methods, and following a new way of his own." This judgment is confirmed by the brief glimpse of the police that the story affords. Their investigation of the theft on which the plot hinges is more reminiscent of Superintendent Seegrave than of Sergeant Cuff: "The one result obtained was the expression of purblind opinion by the authorities of the detective department, which pointed at Isabel [the novel's heroine, a transparently innocent young lady], or at one of the servants, as the undiscovered thief."[33]

According to this view, the police detective, though capable of dealing with the small beer of crime and mystery, proves inadequate to the unusual or unprecedented situation. Yet it was with just such situations that the writers of the age were becoming increasingly concerned—with the plot which originates in the actions of a supremely clever master criminal or the mystery which derives from an abstruse technical point. In such a context the policeman can easily seem a mere blunderer. In "Florence Warden's" *The House on the Marsh* (1884), for example, Maynard is assigned to track down the forger James Woodfall. Woodfall is clearly modeled on Charles Peace, who had been executed for murder five years previously: by day he lives the life of an ordinary country squire, under the name of "Rayner," while at night he works at his coiner's press and carries out daring burglaries in the neighborhood. He is given to talking of "the utter incompetency of the police in the face of a little daring and dexterity," an opinion which the action justifies.[34] After making an elaborately disguised entrance in the best tradition, Maynard is immediately duped: Woodfall gives him a drugged drink and goes out on one of his nocturnal expeditions. During this foray Woodfall is caught, thanks to the exertions of an amateur, and Maynard is given a severe reprimand by his superior:

> The other detective shook him, and glanced at the wine.
> "Drugged," said he shortly.
> With a few vigorous shakes he succeeded in rousing Maynard, and, when he began to look around him in a dazed way, the other said sharply—
> "Pretty fellow you are to be hoodwinked like that, and drink and sleep quietly under the very roof of one of the greatest scoundrels unhung!"
> "Who?" said the other, startled. "Mr. Rayner?"
> "Mr. Rayner! Yes, 'Mr. Rayner' to simple folk like you; but to me and every thief-taker that knows his business— the missing forger, James Woodfall!"[35]

"Amateurs is more harm than good, you may rely on't," complains Inspector Brail in James Payn's *A Confidential Agent* (1880).[36] But it is upon amateurs that the solution depends in that novel, as in *The House on the Marsh*. And it was to amateur or private detectives that writers of the period turned in their growing disillusionment with the police force. Their efforts in this direction were, however, usually tentative and ineffectual. Although the period abandoned the idea of the police detective as hero, it produced no memorable non-police detectives and, until Doyle's work, no equivalent stereotype of the private detective was established.

The failure was accentuated by the foreign examples that lay ready to hand—examples, moreover, in works from which English writers were already beginning to borrow ideas for plot and narrative technique. In his tales of ratiocination Poe, whose own treatment of the police force anticipated some of the English developments of the seventies and eighties, had created a suggestive if sketchy model for the private detective. Dupin is aristocratic in his style of life and social attitudes, eccentric and equipped with a methodology of detection that combines the scientific love of fact and logic with the imagination of the artist. Gaboriau followed Poe's example with Père Tabaret, the unofficial helper of the police originally introduced in *L'Affaire Lerouge* (1866). Inheriting much of Dupin's methodology, Tabaret is essentially a Dupin from a lower level of society and presented in terms of broad comedy. His eccentricities smack of both the vulgar and the manic; the effect is that of a comic zany.

The tentativeness of English writers in adapting or borrowing from such examples is nowhere better illustrated than in Charles Gibbon's *A Hard Knot* (1885), a plagiarized version of *L'Affaire Lerouge*. In certain respects the copy is superior to the original: some of the more laborious parts of Gaboriau's plot are effectively condensed, and the rather vague setting in France is transposed to Glasgow, and given a firm sense of locale. The most radical and least felicitous changes, however, are those affecting the character of the detective. Hadden, the English version of Tabaret, has none of Tabaret's sophisticated methodology: Gaboriau's set pieces displaying the detective's skill in inductive logic are ruthlessly abridged. Following methods that are essentially those of earlier fictional police detectives, Hadden himself is merely a muted and pallid version of the traditional policeman. He is an amiable, ordinary, and solidly respectable figure, who owes little or nothing to his French original.

Wilkie Collins also copied Père Tabaret, in his portrait of Old Sharon in "My Lady's Money." He stays closer to his French model than Gibbon and approaches the experiment with greater verve. The choice of name implicitly acknowledges the debt to Gaboriau, and the point is further enforced by a joking allusion in the scene where Old Sharon first appears. He is found reading a French novel: "There's a dirty old man described in this book that is a little like me . . . Have you read it? A capital story—well put together." Subsequently, he discourses briefly on the "analytical faculty," makes oracular utterances about the mystery—"Suspect, in this case, the

133

very last person on whom suspicion could possibly fall"—and reveals, in a short space of time, a positively alarming number of eccentricities.[37] Yet like Gibbon, Collins follows his French source in a tentative fashion: where Tabaret had dominated the action in which he was involved, Old Sharon makes only two brief appearances, and he does not solve the mystery. The denouement, indeed, provides perhaps the most cloying example of the mysterious ways of Providence in Victorian fiction: the vital missing document on which the plot hinges is accidentally discovered by the heroine's dog.

Although Collins is primarily indebted to Gaboriau's Tabaret, he also takes care to mention that Old Sharon, unlike his French counterpart, has a murky, semicriminal past, being a disbarred lawyer, and is, even as a detective and exponent of the "analytical faculty," a mercenary and untrustworthy character. This harking-back to the older stereotype of the rogue is an almost universal tendency in the presentation of private detectives during this period. Solomon Madgin, in T. W. Speight's *Under Lock and Key* (1869), is a "sly old fox," while Leonidas Lightfoot, in *False Cards*, combines the professions of discreet inquiry agent and charming but unscrupulous confidence trickster.[38]

Disillusioned with the police detective and unable to produce any satisfactory portrait of the professional private detective, the writers of the period often resort to the complete amateur, a character drawn into detection by purely accidental involvement in a mystery or crime. Collins uses the idea in *The Law and the Lady* (1875) and, less successfully, in *"I Say No"* (1884). In *The Moonstone* itself, though the view of the official police is sympathetic, the question of what to do when officialdom fails had already been raised. In the earlier *Woman in White* (1860), in the battle of Walter Hartright and Marion Halcombe against Count Fosco and Sir Perceval Glyde, Collins had made skillful use of the conventional situation of the little men against the big men. The two later books return to the same themes: the central figure is involved in a mystery which the officials of society have failed to solve and have conspired to forget. In each case, significantly, this figure is a woman: Valeria Brinton in *The Law and the Lady* and Emily Brown in *"I Say No."* With his interest in women who refused to conform to the Victorian stereotype of docility and passivity and his craftsman's eye for a suspenseful situation, Collins could not fail to make something of such material. The results are probably the two most interesting of his later novels.

They are, however, more interesting as sidelights on Collins' later career than as episodes in the evolution of a stereotype of the detective. In other writers of the era the use of the amateur detective merely means that his role is conveniently doubled with that of the conventional male romantic lead. With a few gestures toward the theme of detection, the detective is assimilated into pre-existing conventional formulae. The model for this procedure was established by Miss Braddon with the characters of Robert Audley in *Lady Audley's Secret* (1862) and Valentine Hawkehurst in both *Birds of Prey* (1867) and its sequel *Charlotte's Inheritance* (1868). Although these works belong to an earlier period, Miss Braddon's preference for an upper middle-class milieu—her habit of pandering to the snobbish curiosity of her audience—had already led her to create situations in which the intrusion of a professional policeman would have seemed vulgar and irrelevant. The result, in the case of Audley and Hawkehurst, is a version of a familiar Victorian theme: the transformation of an idle young gentleman of pleasure into an earnest, dutiful, and domesticated citizen. Both characters approach the mystery with the gentility's traditional suspicion of detection but soon realize that detection is actually a form of chivalric duty, a course enjoined upon them by family loyalty or romantic attachment. They emerge from the process as fitting mates for the novel's heroines. At the end of *Charlotte's Inheritance* Hawkehurst succeeds in saving the heroine from being murdered by her stepfather: "Fearless as Alcides had he gone down to the realms of darkness; triumphant and glad as a demi-god, he returned from the under-world, bearing his precious burden in his strong arms . . . The struggle had been dire, the agony of suspense a supreme torture; but from the awful contest the man came forth a better and a wiser man."[39]

With an eye for neat commercial formulae Miss Braddon thus produces a convenient solution to the dilemma in which later writers found themselves after the popularity of the police detective had declined. The roles of detective and conventional romantic hero are combined, the details of detective work being subordinated to a stress on chivalric duty and romantic attachment. In a large number of later works— Florence Warden's *The House on the Marsh* is perhaps the best example—the formula recurs with only minor and predictable variations. Young gentlemen free their loved ones from dark clouds overhanging their past, or rescue them from present danger, to be rewarded at the denouement by the heroine's embrace and the prospect of endless domestic bliss. In essence, the formula is far older than Miss Braddon's work, and it is still frequently used in the popular fiction of today.

Thus, though the fiction of the 1870s and 1880s shows a significant change in attitude to the police detective—the dethronement of a minor cultural hero—the result is something of an interregnum. Searching for alternative figures, writers of the era merely returned to older stereotypes, like that of the rogue, or impressed conventional notions of the hero into the service of new needs. The examples of Poe and Gaboriau went largely unheeded. Indeed, reviewing the fiction of this period with the benefit of historical afterknowledge, one finds it difficult to resist the impression that authors were merely marking time until the publication of Doyle's Sherlock Holmes stories. For Doyle's achievement was to create a stereotype of the private detective as complete and as expressive of its time as the earlier stereotype of the police detective had been.

III

FIN DE SIÈCLE

A special product of modern times is the private enquiry agent,
so much employed nowadays, whose ingenuity, patient perti-
nacity, and determination to succeed have been usefully
engaged in unravelling intricate problems, verging upon, if not
actually included within, the realm of crime.

—Major Arthur Griffiths,
Mysteries of Police and Crime (1899)

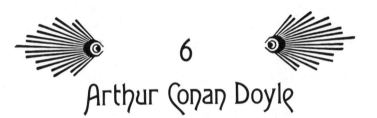

6

Arthur Conan Doyle

It seems possible that Sherlock Holmes is the most famous character in English literature. At any rate, he is certainly a member of that small and oddly assorted group of literary figures—it includes characters as diverse as Hamlet and Robinson Crusoe—whose names and qualities are instantly recognized even by those who have never read the works in which they appear. To successive generations Holmes has been not merely the best-known of fictional detectives but the quintessence of the species: detection in the public mind is a deerstalker, a meerschaum pipe, and an "Elementary, my dear Watson." For subsequent writers in the genre Doyle's work has been at once an inspirational example and an oppressive shadow in which to labor. Modern detective fiction abounds in direct and indirect tribute to Sherlock Holmes, in pale imitations of Doyle's formula and in desperate attempts to break from it.

The security of Holmes's niche in modern English folklore reveals the nature of Doyle's achievement. Earlier writers, like Waters and Gaspey, had made the detective the subject of casual and ephemeral hackwork, or like Godwin and Dickens, they had found in him the crystallization of serious interests. Doyle approached the subject as a workmanlike craftsman determined to write "light fiction" acceptable to an educated public in its moments of relaxation. He even resented the fact that the success of the Holmes stories distracted attention from his "higher work," those historical novels which read like ponderously fictionalized Macaulay.[1] He produced some of the most satisfying middle-brow entertainment of modern times. The Holmes stories maintain a perilous balance: without ever attempting to engage the reader's sensibilities, they manage never to insult his intelligence.

In essence, the formula that underlies the portrayal of Sherlock Holmes is a simple one. The detective is a gentleman, polished and suave in his manners, but reclusive and eccentric in his habits. In his work he is unhampered by official rules, being in a very real sense a law unto himself, and is intensely individualistic. His methods combine the scientist's precision and attention to detail with the flamboyance of the showman and the *preux chevalier's* passion for justice and mercy. In general, the portrait is much like the popular conception of the

140

academic or the intellectual, brilliant and wayward; and it is viewed through the eyes of the worshipful student, represented by the detective's satellite and biographer, Dr. Watson.

Seen in its historical perspective, the portrait of Holmes carries the mid-Victorian respect for the detective to new heights of hero-worship. In other ways, however, it represents a clean break with the stereotype evolved by Waters out of Gaspey and Vidocq, and continued by Dickens and Collins. Holmes is a private detective, not a policeman; a gentleman, not a modestly successful burgher; and is possessed by genius rather than endowed simply with native shrewdness. Doyle supplied the formula for which the writers of the 1870s and 1880s, in their disillusion with the police detective, had been fumbling. Moreover, as the success which was accorded his work in his day shows, he had created a figure uniquely attractive to the public for light reading. Sherlock Holmes, it may be said, was a cliché whose time had come; he was, contemporaries felt, the perfect hero for his age.

The origins of Doyle's formula lay partly in his own past. Holmes is suggestive of a brilliant but eccentric professor seen through the eyes of an admiring student because, as Doyle indicated, his conception of the detective owed much to his memories of Dr. Joseph Bell, a lecturer who had impressed him during his undergraduate years at Edinburgh University. Doyle explained that while planning *A Study in Scarlet* (1887), the first work in which Holmes appears, "I thought of my old teacher Joe Bell, of his eagle face, of his curious ways, of his eerie trick of spotting details. If he were a detective he would surely reduce this fascinating but unorganized business to something nearer to an exact science."[2] Sherlock Holmes inherits that gift for startling diagnosis which had so impressed Dr. Bell's undergraduate audiences. At his first meeting with Watson the detective's greeting is a laconic, "You have been in Afghanistan, I perceive" (*CLS*, 10).[3] In "The Red-Headed League" (1891) he comments to his friend on their client, Jabez Wilson: "Beyond the obvious facts that he has at some time done manual labour, that he takes snuff, that he is a Freemason, that he has been in China, and that he has done a considerable amount of writing lately, I can deduce nothing else"

(CCS, 31). In most of the stories Holmes performs a similar feat as the prelude to his solution of the main problem; he flaunts his credentials for the benefit of reader and client alike.

Yet too much importance should not be attached to Dr. Bell as the real-life model for Holmes. Bell's methods of observation and deduction would have been sufficiently familiar to most doctors and scientists of the age. It was rather his theatrical way of presenting the results which was distinctive, and which Holmes inherits. The detective's main characteristics have obvious literary precedents. Reacting against the earlier stereotype of the policeman hero, Doyle reverted boldly to the example of Poe and Gaboriau, to the Chevalier Dupin and his literary progeny, M. Lecoq and Père Tabaret.

Like Holmes, Dupin had been used as the recurrent hero of a series of stories; and he too was presented through the eyes of an admiring friend. Dupin also shared a discreetly respectable birth, "of an excellent—indeed of an illustrious family." His tastes were recondite and erudite: he originally encountered the narrator of the stories through "the accident of our both being in search of the same very rare and very remarkable volume" in "an obscure library in the Rue Montmartre." He lived with the narrator in a "perfect" seclusion, which he carried to the extent of excluding daylight from his rooms and venturing outside only at night.[4] And Dupin's approach to detection was based, more solidly than that of any preceding detective, on the assumptions of scientific rationalism.

Doyle acknowledged his debt to Poe with typical generosity: "M. Dupin had from boyhood been one of my heroes," he explained in *Memories and Adventures*.[5] But the point had already been made as early as *A Study in Scarlet*. When Watson, astounded by his friend's newly revealed powers, admiringly compares him to Dupin, Holmes contemptuously retorts: "Now, in my opinion, Dupin was a very inferior fellow. That trick of his of breaking in on his friend's thoughts with an apropos remark after a quarter of an hour's silence is really very showy and superficial. He had some analytical genius, no doubt; but he was by no means such a phenomenon as Poe appeared to imagine" (CLS, 23). He goes on to abuse Gaboriau's Monsieur Lecoq in similar terms. The joke, of course, is on Holmes. At the beginning of a later story, "The Card-board Box" (1893), he practices that trick of thought-reading which he had earlier denounced: by silently observing Watson, he is able to trace an elaborate train of association beginning with an unframed portrait of Henry Ward Beecher and ending with melancholy reflections of the absurdity of war. Holmes's chain of reasoning is no more persuasive than Dupin's had been in "The Murders in the Rue Morgue," but Doyle was obviously pleased with it: when he decided to omit "The Cardboard Box" from *The Memoirs of Sherlock Holmes,* he grafted the thought-reading scene on to the beginning of "The Resident Patient" (1893), where it is still sometimes printed.

Similar examples of details borrowed from the portrait of Dupin—and other Poe characters—are scattered throughout the Holmes stories. The narrator of "The Murders in the Rue Morgue" "often dwelt meditatively upon the old philosophy of the Bi-Part soul, and amused myself with the fancy of a double Dupin."[6] Watching his friend relax at a concert after grappling with the problem of "The Red-Headed League," Watson notes in him a "dual nature" (*CSS,* 45), an alternation between extreme energy and extreme lassitude. Like Dupin, Holmes lures suspects to his rooms by artfully worded newspaper advertisements; like Legrand in "The Gold Bug," he is an expert at cryptography; and like the anonymous narrator of "The Man of the Crowd," he has the knack of deducing people's occupations from their physical appearance.

When, near the beginning of *A Study in Scarlet,* Watson records that Holmes has a habit of melancholic and unmelodious improvisation on his violin, the reader is irresistibly reminded of Roderick Usher and his guitar. But Holmes commonly concludes his impromptu meditations on the violin with a gesture most unlike Usher, playing a series of Watson's favorite tunes "as a slight compensation for the trial upon my patience" (*CLS, Study in Scarlet,* 18). The effect is to remind the reader that, despite their obvious similarities, the world of Poe and the world of Doyle are ultimately far apart. Doyle took from Poe the general outline and several specific details of the detective's character, but he uses them only as a starting point, and a starting point for quite different effects. His stories have none of Poe's striving after profundity and none of Poe's intensity of manner; his tone is relaxed and genial, and his aim is always to reassure and entertain the reader.

Many of the details that Doyle borrows from Poe are thus suffused with an atmosphere of cosiness entirely alien to the spirit of the earlier writer. Dupin, for example, inveighed against the stupidity of policemen, reporters, and witnesses with an antidemocratic stridency. His detection, like those practical jokes and hoaxes which Poe loved, was a passionate exercise in proving his superiority to the ordinary man. Humbler spirits, like the Prefect of Police in "The Purloined Letter," retreated humbled and chagrined by the detective's supreme cleverness.

Doyle handles the detective's superiority to his fellows entirely differently. Holmes continually outstrips both Watson and policemen like Lestrade and Gregson. His battle of wits with the police, however, shows not genuine antagonism but the friendly rivalry of long-acquainted sparring partners. At one point, in fact, Lestrade bursts into an affectionate, unsolicited testimonial for the private detective:

> "I've seen you handle a good many cases, Mr. Holmes, but I don't know that I ever knew a more workmanlike one than that. We're not jealous of you at Scotland Yard. No, sir, we are very proud of you, and if you come down to-morrow there's not a man, from the oldest inspector to the youngest constable, who wouldn't be glad to shake you by the hand."
>
> "Thank you!" said Holmes. "Thank you!" and as he turned away it seemed to me that he was more nearly moved by the softer human emotions than I had ever seen him. (CSS, "Six Napoleons," 762–763)

Such sentimentality had no precedent in Poe. Similarly, the edge of Holmes's more general expressions of contempt for ordinary people is blunted by touches of comedy. His apostrophes of Watson's dimness are comic scenes, expressions of a harmless, even endearing vanity which is part of the great man's make-up. When Holmes chooses to abuse the public at large, he does so in a manner very different from Dupin: "Pshaw, my dear fellow, what do the public, the great unobservant public, who could hardly tell a weaver by his tooth or a compositor by his left thumb, care about the finer shades of analysis and deduction!" (*CSS*, "Copper Beeches," 276).

The difference between Poe and Doyle on this issue might be explained by the fact that the one was a tolerant and broad-minded English gentleman while the other strove hard to play the role of dignified Southern aristocrat. The more general difference in tone between the two *oeuvres* can be accounted for by the fact that Doyle was a middle-brow writer of modest literary ambitions, whereas Poe was a serious artist working in the mainstream of the Romantic tradition. It seems likely, however, that Doyle's variations on his source were owing in part to a more specific factor: he had read Robert Louis Stevenson's tales and fantasies and been influenced by the manner in which they assimilated and adapted material from Poe.

A strong debt to Stevenson is apparent in Doyle's work as a whole, not merely in the Sherlock Holmes stories. In his historical and adventure fiction Doyle strove hard to create that atmosphere of open-air masculinity of which Stevenson was the contemporary master. Stevenson also wrote a number of books which reveal a circumspect flirting with detective themes. Several of these were published after the creation of Sherlock Holmes, but two were early enough to have influenced Doyle's own approach: *The New Arabian Nights* (1882) and *The Dynamiter* (1885). The first of these books, a loose collection of fantastic and comic stories, dealt with the adventures of Prince Florizel, a suave and courteous monarch who explored the underside of London life and encountered various crimes and injustices he proceeded to punish in a melodramatic fashion. The second book, hardly more unified than the first, was apparently inspired by the Fenian bomb attacks in London, for it had a passionate Preface denouncing the saboteurs. In content, however, it was very like its predecessor. Prince Florizel, now dethroned and turned tobacconist, had become a minor character, and the heroes were a trio of gullible young men who embarked on a series of comic adventures in the persuasion that detection was "the only profession for a gentleman."[7]

From these stories Doyle took a number of hints. He used one of the interpolated stories in *The Dynamiter* as the basis for the lengthy Mormon episode which occupies the latter part of

A Study in Scarlet.[8] The portrait of Florizel himself provided a model for a genteel detective less extreme and more personable than Poe's Dupin: Florizel was charming and courtly, whereas Dupin was nervous and strident.

Above all, Doyle was influenced by Stevenson's style of writing, a mannered approach which often strained too hard to charm the reader but which aimed at a tone of sunny good temper. This style lent itself readily to a vein of fantasy very different from Poe's use of the bizarre and grotesque. It was whimsical rather than morbid in spirit, and it dealt with situations that were intended to be striking rather than frightening. It was exemplified by *The New Arabian Nights* in scenes such as that of the eccentric young man distributing tarts in the public house, and in ideas such as that of the club for would-be suicides. Similar fantastic ideas abound in the Holmes stories and account for much of their atmosphere of light-hearted comedy. In this respect at least one of the tales, "The Red-Headed League," is a minor masterpiece. Holmes's interest in this adventure is originally kindled by hearing the story of Jabez Wilson who, on the strength of the color of his hair, has been employed by the league of red-headed men to copy out the contents of the *Encyclopaedia Britannica*.

In his conception of Sherlock Holmes, Doyle was also influenced by a tradition of nineteenth century literature, influential in its own time yet largely forgotten today: the tradition of biography, especially eulogistic biography, launched with the publication of Boswell's *Life of Johnson* in 1791. From the beginning of the saga Doyle's interest in character is greater than his interest in theory: Holmes is presented as a great man in his own right and not just as the incarnation of a particular methodology of detection. The stories do not merely relate a succession of criminal cases, but also chronicle the growth of both the friendship between Holmes and Watson and the detective's own career, from his days as an undergraduate, through a period of international recognition, to his serene retirement on the south coast.

The form which this chronicle takes, a narrative by an admiring satellite of the hero, echoes the device which Poe adopted in the Dupin tales. It is superbly appropriate to the structural requirements of detective fiction. But it also echoes the central situation of Boswell's *Life of Johnson* and of many succeeding biographies in the nineteenth century. Noting the parallel with Boswell's work, Richard Altick has catalogued the various ways in which Holmes resembles Dr. Johnson: both are given to dogmatic and sometimes prejudiced opinions, to a covert love of praise, to bouts of melancholy, and to a love of conversation.[9] Often Holmes' utterances show an epigrammatic neatness distinctly reminiscent of Johnson. In *The Hound of the Baskervilles* (1901–1902), for example, he remarks: "It is my experience that it is only an amiable man in this world who receives testimonials, only an unambitious one who abandons a London career for the country, and only an absent-minded one who leaves his stick and not his visiting-card after waiting an hour in your room" (*CLS*, 279). Holmes, as Altick has also noted, is in the habit of referring to Watson as his "Boswell," while Doyle himself, as he acknowledged in *Through the Magic Door*, was an ardent Johnsonian.[10]

Doyle was apparently glancing over his shoulder not merely at Boswell's *Life* but at the whole spate of biographies which appeared during the nineteenth century. In the Victorian era, friends and relatives rushed to memorialize their dead in print; volumes of reminiscences or more ambitious three-volume "lives and letters" were almost as common and natural a tribute to the departed great as black crepe and funeral wreaths. This love of biography was briefly satirized in Collins' *The Moonstone* through the portrait of Miss Clack, the Evangelical spinster, with her copy of *The Life, Letters, and Labours of Miss Jane Ann Stamper*. The best examples of the form, like John Lockhart's life of Scott and Forster's life of Dickens, are still read today; Doyle himself was the subject of a weaker and more representative specimen, the *Memoir* by his fellow spiritualist, Rev. John Lamond.

Watson himself, prematurely chronicling Holmes's death in "The Final Problem" (1893), strikes a sonorous note typical of the genre. He begins, "It is with a heavy heart that I take up my pen to write these the last words in which I shall ever record the singular gifts by which my friend Mr. Sherlock Holmes was distinguished" (*CSS*, 536). The story concludes, with an allusion to Socrates' tribute to Plato, by referring to Holmes as "him whom I shall ever regard as the best and wisest man whom I have ever known" (CSS, 556).

These echoes of contemporary biography explain Doyle's playful attempts to persuade the reader of Holmes's actual existence, a game which Baker Street scholars of the present day have been only too ready to continue. At the beginning of "The Speckled Band" (1892) Watson explains that the story can now be told since its heroine has recently died, while the story of "The Engineer's Thumb" (1892) has "been told more than once in the newspapers" (CSS, 201). The case of "The Veiled Lodger" (1927) is prefaced by an account of attempts to destroy various papers relating to Holmes's cases, now in Watson's possession: "The source of these outrages is known, and if they are repeated I have Mr. Holmes's authority for saying that the whole story concerning the politician, the lighthouse, and the trained cormorant will be given to the public" (CSS, 1288).

Several of these references to unnarrated cases which are scattered throughout the stories associate Holmes with real figures. The detective is made a member of the Legion of Honor and receives an autographed letter from the French President for his arrest of Huret, the boulevard assassin. At the request of the Pope he investigates the "little affair of the Vatican cameos" (CLS, Hound of the Baskervilles, 289). It is broadly hinted that the title character of "The Illustrious Client" (1925) is King Edward VII and that Holmes is rewarded for his work in "The Bruce-Partington Plans" (1908) by an audience with Queen Victoria. To complete the real-life effect, Watson in a Preface to the penultimate collection of stories, His Last Bow (1917), gives a glimpse of Holmes in his twilight years which reads like an entry in an alumni magazine: "The friends of Mr. Sherlock Holmes will be glad to learn that he is alive and well, though somewhat crippled by occasional attacks of rheumatism. He has, for many years, lived in a small farm upon the downs five miles from Eastbourne, where his time is divided between philosophy and agriculture."[11]

The stories also contain veiled and playful allusions to the larger issues which the nineteenth century habit of biography and reminiscence raised in contemporary minds. Many eminent men were angry at the prospect of posthumous invasions of their privacy. Both Tennyson and Dickens, for example, destroyed important letters and papers.[12] In the Holmes stories the detective shows a similar "aversion to publicity" (*CSS*, "Devil's Foot," 1040), which can frustrate Watson's attempts to memorialize him. He is secretive about his background, having known Watson for several years before mentioning that he has a brother, Mycroft, and he is often reluctant to give permission for his cases to be chronicled. At the beginning of "The Devil's Foot" (1910) Watson exultantly records the receipt of a telegram from the detective in retirement licensing publication of the details of the Cornish horror: "I have no idea what backward sweep of memory had brought the matter fresh to his mind, or what freak had caused him to desire that I should recount it; but I hasten, before another cancelling telegram may arrive, to hunt out the notes which give me exact details of the case and to lay the narrative before my readers" (*CSS*, 1041).

Similarly, readers and writers of the age were disturbed about how many of the subject's defects a biographer should reveal. The issue had been raised in an acute form by James Froude's remarkably—and to some, offensively—frank life of his friend Carlyle.[13] In his essay on Dr. Johnson in *Through the Magic Door*, Doyle supported candid biography in the style of Boswell, and it is this policy that Holmes, despite his vanity, urges on his friend: "Watson, Watson, if you are an honest man you will record this also and set it against my successes!" (*CLS*, 312) he exclaims in *The Hound of the Baskervilles* after having lost the trail of a suspect.

The fact that Holmes, unlike the subject of the usual Victorian biography, remains alive to comment on his chronicler's activities allows Doyle further opportunity for humorous commentary on the form. The stories become, at times, running accounts of the tribulations of a biographer's life. Holmes remains alive not merely to control what Watson may or may not publish, but to comment disparagingly on the results. Most succinct in this respect is his reproof to Watson in "The Abbey Grange" (1904): "Your fatal habit of looking at everything from the point of view of a story instead of as a scientific exercise has ruined what might have been an instructive and even classical series of demonstrations. You slur over work of the utmost finesse and delicacy in order to dwell upon sensational details which may excite but cannot possibly instruct the reader" (CSS, 834).

Although many of Doyle's references to the tradition of Victorian biography are parodic, he is in one respect entirely in sympathy with the impulses underlying the form. To the Victorians, biography was pre-eminently a eulogistic genre, and its popularity, as Richard Altick has argued, "cannot be explained without reference to the fashion—one might indeed say institution—of hero-worship."[14] Thackeray, in the course of an essay on Swift, declared that he would have loved to be Shakespeare's bootboy, and the Holmes stories invite the reader to indulge a similar fantasy of being the initiate, in however humble a capacity, of a great man. Watson, with whom the reader is encouraged to identify, is at once proud of his intimacy with Holmes and respectfully conscious of the gap that separates them. This gap is caused as much by the inimitable nature of Holmes's greatness as by his reticence. But Watson has a function, and one that satisfies him: to record and publicize the exploits of his hero. In return he is rewarded with an invigorating contact with greatness and with occasional glimpses of the affection which the great man feels for him:

> "You're not hurt, Watson? For God's sake, say that you are not hurt!"
> It was worth a wound—it was worth many wounds—to know the depth of loyalty and love which lay behind that cold mask. The clear, hard eyes were dimmed for a moment, and the firm lips were shaking. For the one and only time I caught a glimpse of a great heart as well as of a great brain. All my years of humble but single-minded service culminated in that moment of revelation.
> "It's nothing, Holmes. It's a mere scratch." (CSS, "Three Garridebs," 1213)

So far Sherlock Holmes has been spoken of as a fixed entity, and the stories as a continuous chronicle or saga. Yet their appearance spanned some forty years, beginning with *A Study in Scarlet* in 1887 and ending with the book publication of the last *Strand* magazine stories, *The Case-Book of Sherlock Holmes,* in 1927. As Doyle himself remarked in the Preface to *His Last Bow,* Holmes lived through three eras: the late Victorian, the Edwardian, and the Georgian. Doyle did not intend that Holmes's career should be so lengthy, and the chronicle inevitably has a haphazard and extemporaneous air: there are enough inconsistencies to have sustained a minor industry of mock scholarly exegesis and speculation.

The characterization of Sherlock Holmes also changes, reflecting the development of Doyle's own values as well as the different tastes of the various eras in which the stories first appeared. For the purposes of analysis the canon may be divided into three periods. The first of these is represented by *A Study in Scarlet* and *The Sign of Four* (1890), the earliest and weakest of the full-length novels. Here Holmes is not merely a less fully realized creation than he later becomes but is also more inhumanly dedicated to the principles of science and more tinged with Decadence. The second period begins with the series of short stories appearing in the *Strand* between July 1891 and June 1892, published in volume form as *The Adventures of Sherlock Holmes* (1892). In these tales and their immediate successors, *The Memoirs of Sherlock Holmes* (1894), Doyle found his true métier and his true audience: they are the best and most popular of his work. The Holmes of this period is more calculated to appeal to a middle-class readership than the earlier figure. He is moved as much by a passion for justice and a sense of *noblesse oblige* as by a love of scientific truth or artistic form. The final period, beginning in 1901 with Holmes's reappearance in *The Hound of the Baskervilles,* is one of progressive decline. By the time of the *Strand* stories, collected as *The Return of Sherlock Holmes* (1905), *His Last Bow,* and *The Case-Book of Sherlock Holmes,* the detective has become a more crudely drawn and less impressive figure than earlier.

From the beginning of *A Study in Scarlet* its hero is identified as a scientist, even before either the narrator or the reader is aware of the specific nature of his profession. By the time Holmes reveals to Watson, at the end of the second chapter, that he is a "consulting detective" (*CLS,* 21), the point has already been firmly established that detection is actually an extension of scientific principles into the practical affairs of men. Standish, who introduces Holmes and Watson, merely describes the detective as a "fellow who is working at the chemical laboratory up at the hospital" (*CLS*, 7), and it is in this setting that Holmes is first seen, playing the role of Archimedes:

> This was a lofty chamber, lined and littered with countless bottles. Broad, low tables were scattered about, which bristled with retorts, test-tubes, and little Bunsen lamps, with their blue flickering flames. There was only one student in the room, who was bending over a distant table absorbed in his work. At the sound of our steps he glanced round and sprang to his feet with a cry of pleasure. "I've found it! I've found it," he shouted to his companion, running towards us with a test-tube in his hand. "I have found a reagent which is precipitated by haemoglobin, and by nothing else." Had he discovered a gold mine, greater delight could not have shone upon his features. (*CLS*, 10)

Shortly afterward, the list of Holmes's accomplishments compiled by Dr. Watson in an attempt to discover the detective's profession describes his knowledge of chemistry as "profound" (*CLS*, 18). Several of the subsequent stories smack of the laboratory. In *The Sign of Four*, for example, Holmes distracts himself with chemical experiments when his investigations into the murder of Bartholomew Sholto have reached an impasse, and a later adventure, "The Naval Treaty" (1893), begins in a manner reminiscent of the introduction of Holmes in *A Study in Scarlet*.

Despite Doyle's determination to impress the picture of Holmes as a working scientist upon the reader, these laboratory scenes have a distinctly factitious air. Only in the passage from *A Study in Scarlet* is the object of the chemical test indicated with any exactitude. None of the scenes, moreover, is integral to the action of the story: Holmes's solution of his cases never depends on precise scientific details in the manner of, say, Austin Freeman's Dr. Thorndyke. Doyle is primarily interested in the superficially dramatic possibilities of the laboratory. The episodes are designed to impress the reader, as they do Watson, with a sense of Holmes's powers; the effect is largely dependent on the vagueness of the reference.

The stories' relation to the details of contemporary science is tenuous.[15] Holmes himself utters very unscientific judgments. In "The Blue Carbuncle" (1892) he bases a deduction on the idea that a man's intellectual capacities are reflected in his head size, while in "The Marzarin Stone" (1921) he defends his abstention from food during periods of intense work on the grounds that "the faculties become refined when you starve them" (CSS, 1143). Dr. Watson, surprisingly, accepts this argument without demur. Nor are the references to criminological science more exact. In *The Hound of the Baskervilles*, the French scientist Alphonse Bertillon is referred to as the greatest contemporary criminological authority. Yet at the time the novel was published (1901–1902), Bertillon's work was largely obsolescent: his main contribution to criminology, an elaborate system of measurements designed to identify criminals, had proved cumbersome and was being superseded by the fingerprint system.[16] Of fingerprinting there is only one mention in the Holmes stories, in "The Norwood Builder" (1903): here the detective treats the new system with disdain and shows that the police have been misled by their excessive faith in it.

In its general outline, however, Holmes's approach to detection participates intimately in that spirit of scientific rationalism which had come to dominate the intellectual climate of the late Victorian period. His use of disguise would have reminded contemporaries of Vidocq, as his interest in footprints would have recalled Gaboriau's hero, Lecoq. Above all, Holmes would have seemed to contemporary readers the successor to the methods of Cuvier, of Darwin, and of Huxley. The stories convert some of the most complex and disturbing issues of the period into the material for beguiling romance. For this effort of *haute vulgarisation* Doyle was peculiarly well equipped. Coming from a traditionally Roman Catholic family, he had been exposed to the methods and assumptions of contemporary science through his studies at Edinburgh University. As his autobiography records, the work of Huxley and Tyndall had shaken his religious faith. Doyle's suggestion that he began *A Study in Scarlet* by asking what Joseph Bell would have done if he had been a detective may give an exaggerated notion of the doctor's influence on Holmes's character, but as a metaphor for the underlying intention of the stories, which was to popularize scientific method, it is superbly exact.

Much of the work of nineteenth century science was directed toward the reconstruction of past events. By following the principles of inductive logic and noting the similar patterns of causation, scientists found in contemporary reality evidence of the prehistory of the world. Darwin could draw conclusions about the mechanisms by which species adapt from his observation of pigeons, as Cuvier could reconstruct the anatomy of prehistoric animals from a few surviving bones. The method received its most succinct exemplification in Huxley's lecture of 1868 to an audience of working men, "On a Piece of Chalk." Beginning with his lecturer's chalk, Huxley was able to work back to a complex geological map of the world's surface in prehuman times. The detail of contemporary life, the piece of chalk, spoke volumes of prehistory: "A small beginning has led us to a great ending."[17]

Huxley's method is specifically echoed in Holmes's article "The Book of Life," quoted near the beginning of A Study in Scarlet: "From a drop of water . . . a logician could infer the possibility of an Atlantic or a Niagara without having seen or heard of one or the other. So all life is a great chain, the nature of which is known whenever we are shown a single link of it" (CLS, 20). In Holmes's work, as in that of contemporary scientists, the ability to get at the truth of things resides, in Walter Pater's phrase, in "a power of distinguishing and fixing delicate and fugitive detail."[18] Whereas the scientists applied the method to the murky prehistory of the world, Holmes uses it to reconstruct mysterious criminal events. From the apparent trivia found at the scene of a crime he is able to draw dramatic and far-reaching conclusions. "Dear me, Watson," he chides his long-suffering colleague in The Valley of Fear (1914–1915), "is it possible that you have not penetrated the fact that the case hangs upon the missing dumb-bell?" (CLS, 516).

Taking their cue from Holmes's method, the stories themselves show a minute precision of description, a supreme attentiveness to the surface of life. The opening of The Hound of the Baskervilles gives a detailed account of the sort of walking stick a country doctor would be likely to own, while "The Bruce-Partington Plans" describes what a clerk at the Navy Office might be expected to carry in his pockets on an ordinary day. Holmes's deductions allow the reader to find a meaning and an interest in such apparently mundane items. Just as Huxley had taught his audience to look at a piece of chalk with new interest, so Holmes teaches Watson and the reader to look upon the ordinary trivia of the physical world with renewed vision. Such trivia become the subjects of miniature romances, small human histories: the man's hat in "The Blue Carbuncle" is made to tell a short sentimental tale of an unhappy marriage, while Watson's watch in *The Sign of Four* reveals a melodramatic chapter in the Watson family history.

To contemporaries, much of the attraction of Holmes would have resided in his ability to convey a sense of excitement about the ordinary physical world which they inhabited. His attentiveness to things does not merely refresh the spectator's vision; it imparts a sense of control. The scientific rationalists of the age insisted that their discoveries led to a new vision of human power. Winwood Reade, a writer to whom Holmes several times refers, claimed in *The Martyrdom of Man:* "When we have ascertained, by means of Science, the methods of Nature's operation, we shall be able to take her place, and to perform them for ourselves . . . men will master the forces of Nature; they will become themselves the architects of systems, manufacturers of worlds."[19] Within the simpler and less demanding confines of his own fictional world, Holmes becomes just such a master of his environment. "He loved to lie in the very centre of five millions of people," Watson observes, "with his filaments stretching out and running through them, responsive to every little rumour or suspicion of unsolved crimes" (*CSS*, "Cardboard Box," 924). Before his omniscience the terrors of the world lose their sting. "What danger do you foresee?" Miss Hunter asks him in "The Copper Beeches" (1892): "Holmes shook his head gravely. 'It would cease to be a danger if we could define it,' said he" (*CSS*, 283–284).

Holmes several times performs the archetypal role of the rationalist hero: he explodes superstitions and frees people from their influence. In "The Sussex Vampire" (1924) he explains a case of supposed vampirism, and in "The Devil's Foot" he tackles the notion of demonic possession. In *The Hound of the Baskervilles*, the most successful of the full-length novels, he shows that the apparently all-powerful hound of hell is merely a phosphorous-painted dog which can be killed with real bullets.[20]

Holmes's scientism, stressed throughout the stories, helps to make him a fitting hero for his age. But in the earliest stories the intensity of his dedication to science can also make him a suspect and repellent figure. It is not that he approaches criminal and human problems with a methodology drawn from contemporary science. To him, criminals and human problems are simply scientific puzzles, opportunities for a display of expertise. He is motivated solely by a passion for scientific truth; the fact that his work may serve the interests of justice, or that it may have painful human consequences, is of no concern to him. Standish, describing Holmes before his appearance in *A Study in Scarlet,* sounds an important note of warning: "Holmes is a little too scientific for my tastes—it approaches to cold-bloodedness. I could imagine his giving a friend a little pinch of the latest vegetable alkaloid, not out of malevolence, you understand, but simply out of a spirit of inquiry in order to have a more accurate idea of the effects. To do him justice, I think he would take it himself with the same readiness" (CLS, 9). This habit of mind is seen in action in *The Sign of Four,* when Holmes deduces from the watch which Watson has inherited from his brother a sad story of alcoholism and wasted talents. Intensely bound up in the problem in its purely scientific light, he suddenly pulls himself up and apologizes to Watson: "Viewing the matter as an abstract problem I had forgotten how personal and painful a thing it might be to you" (CLS, 150).

This impression of a somewhat inhuman detachment from ordinary social values—from those values so solidly represented by Watson—is furthered by the overtones of Decadence which surround Holmes and his work in the two early novels.[21] These books were written at a time when aestheticism was firmly established and Decadence was coming into fashion in literary circles; they draw upon this atmosphere in much the same way as they do upon the scientific and rationalist temper of the age. Doyle's relation to the Decadent movement is neatly epitomized by the genesis of *The Sign of*

Four. The idea for a second Holmes novel was suggested to him by the American publisher Lippincott; Doyle agreed to the project at a dinner party at which Oscar Wilde entered into a similar undertaking to write *The Portrait of Dorian Gray*.[22]

At times, the reader of *The Sign of Four* may be forgiven for wondering if Doyle was deliberately trying to take a leaf of his fellow author's work, so directly does the novel employ the appurtenances which Decadence had made fashionable. His detective is a recluse who holds himself aloof from ordinary men and ordinary existence; he alternates between bouts of nervous excitement and moods of dreamy languor in which he falls prey to melancholy brooding, consoles himself with extravagant extemporizations on the violin, or takes refuge (much to Watson's alarm) in a world of fantasy induced by cocaine. Doyle may have borrowed hints for the detective's eccentric habits from Poe; but he elaborated them in the light of what Poe's spiritual heirs, the Decadents of the late 1880s, had contributed to the myth of the sensitive genius.

With its reference to the terminology of Impressionist painting and its hint of the bizarre, the title of *A Study in Scarlet* would have appealed to Wilde and his contemporaries. The phrase is suggested by Holmes himself when he describes the book's main murder mystery as "the finest study I ever came across: a study in scarlet, eh? Why shouldn't we use a little art jargon? There's the scarlet thread of murder running through the colourless skein of life, and our duty is to unravel it, and isolate it, and expose every inch of it" (*CLS*, 44). The use of "a little art jargon" is characteristic, for the Holmes of the early period regards detection as an art to be practiced for its own sake. Crime appeals not merely to the scientist's instinct for the puzzle but to the Decadent's love of "all that is bizarre and outside the conventions and humdrum routine of everyday life" (*CSS*, "Red-Headed League," 29). Detection brings the artist that excitement in the exercise of his own powers which daily life commonly denies. "My life," Holmes tells Watson at the end of "The Red-Headed League," "is spent in one long effort to escape from the commonplace of existence. These little problems help me to do so" (*CSS*, 55). The effect of this rigidly aesthetic appraoch is much like that of the purely scientific attitude: seen as an activity to be pursued for its own sake, detection becomes divorced from any moral or social perspective.

Doyle's interest in Decadence, however, was of another caliber from his interest in scientific rationalism. His photograph shows him to have been the epitome of the military-looking, tweedy English gentleman; it bears a striking likeness to the reader's mental image of Dr. Watson. His life shows him to have been closer in temperament to the anti-Decadents than to the Decadents. He defended the conduct of the English troops in the Boer War, patronized amateur sport, and derided feminism. His favorite contemporary writer appears to have been Rudyard Kipling. Although he apparently liked Wilde as a person and wrote of his homosexuality with a surprising lack of cant, Doyle would no doubt have regarded the Decadent movement with much the same horror that modernism inspired in him. He belonged to a class of Englishmen who have traditionally had little time for dangerous, arty nonsense.

It therefore seems likely that he added the touches of Decadence to the characterization of the early Holmes in order to strike a topical note, and perhaps to gain a little of the publicity which Wilde and his colleagues were so adept at attracting. But by the mid-1890s and the trial of Wilde, Decadence would have been not merely less novel but dangerously associated with scandalous matters. Correspondingly, Holmes's Decadence is progressively muted after the two early novels. He continues to be attracted by bizarre details and to express a peevish anger at the commonplaceness of existence, as in "The Norwood Builder," where he is even sufficiently antisocial to lament that the death of Moriarty has taken the fun out of detection. But the cocaine, surely Holmes's most blatant venture into Decadence, all but disappears after *The Sign of Four*; it is briefly alluded to in "A Scandal in Bohemia" (1891), the next story in the sequence, and in "The Missing Three-Quarter" (1904), where Watson expresses a passing fear that "the fiend was not dead, but sleeping" (CSS, 809). Whereas the early Holmes was wont to retreat into narcotic fantasy at the end of a case, the later Holmes is more likely to propose that he and Watson dine at a fashionable restaurant or spend an evening together at the opera.

Although the detective continues to speak of his detection as an art to be practiced for its own sake, the phrase takes on more innocuous connotations: it usually means simply that he is not interested in financial reward or public praise. In "The Bruce-Partington Plans" the idea is translated into terms more comprehensible and acceptable to the ordinary rugger-playing Englishman: "I play the game for the game's own sake" (*CSS*, 975). The main surviving evidence of Holmes's artistic temperament is his love of creating flamboyant and surprising effects, a habit more reminiscent of Poe's Dupin than of the Decadent artist, and one that has little to do with "art" except in the broadest sense of the term. Holmes surprises clients with on-the-spot deductions and arranges for artfully contrived denouements to his cases. At one such moment, in *The Valley of Fear*, the detective playfully lectures his stolid policeman colleague in tones reminiscent of Thomas De Quincey arguing for artistry in crime:

> "Watson insists that I am the dramatist in real life," said he. "Some touch of the artist wells up within me and calls insistently for a well-staged performance. Surely our profession, Mr. Mac, would be a drab and sordid one if we did not sometimes set the scene so as to glorify our results. The blunt accusation, the brutal tap upon the shoulder—what can one make of such a *dénouement*? But the quick inference, the subtle trap, the clever forecast of coming events, the triumphant vindication of bold theories—are these not the pride and the justification of our life's work? At the present moment you thrill with the glamour of the situation and the anticipation of the hunt." (*CLS*, 533)

As this severe modification of Holmes's Decadent tendencies would suggest, the detective becomes in general a more conventional figure than he had originally been. He becomes, it might be said, more like Watson. During the middle period, beginning with publication of the first short stories in the *Strand* in July 1891 and lasting until 1893, Doyle's characterization of Holmes was no doubt heavily influenced by the new readership to which the detective had been introduced. Reginald Pound, historian of the *Strand*, has noted: "Certainly the middle-classes of England never cast a clearer image of themselves in print than they did in *The Strand Magazine*. Confirming their preference for mental as well as physical comfort, for more than half a century it faithfully mirrored their tastes, prejudices, and intellectual limitations. From them it drew a large and loyal readership that was the envy of the publishing world."[23]

The assimilation of Holmes into this format begins with a change in his physical appearance. In *A Study in Scarlet* Holmes had been described in the following manner:

> His very person and appearance were such as to strike the attention of the most casual observer. In height he was rather over six feet, and so excessively lean that he seemed to be considerably taller. His eyes were sharp and piercing, save during those intervals of torpor to which I have alluded; and his thin, hawk-like nose gave his whole expression an air of alertness and decision. His chin, too, had the prominence and squareness which mark the man of determination. His hands were invariably blotted with ink and stained with chemicals, yet he was possessed of extraordinary delicacy of touch, as I frequently had occasion to observe when I watched him manipulating his fragile philosophical instruments. (*CLS*, 15)

This is very different from the physical image of Holmes that emerges from the *Strand* stories. Doyle at that time usually avoided describing him in detail, but he did give tacit consent to the Sidney Paget engravings. These portray a figure very different from the powerful but ugly hero of *A Study in Scarlet*: handsome, intellectual, elegantly slim rather than "excessively lean," and given to mildly dandified poses. When Doyle does refer to Holmes's appearance in the stories, it is in a way consonant with Paget's drawings: the reader glimpses his aquiline profile, his enigmatic smile, and his brooding eyes. He is not merely a striking but a suavely commanding figure.

A certain suavity also enters Holmes's social manners. In the early period, Holmes had been the living embodiment of Dr. Johnson's unclubbable man, a difficult and irritating person for Watson to live with. In the *Strand* stories the nervous excitability, the fits of melancholy, and the flashes of vanity remain; but Holmes has also become more charming and personable. In his dialogues with Watson before or after a case—and these occupy a surprisingly large part of each story—he develops a vein of pleasantly whimsical humor. In his treatment of strangers, visitors, and clients he is customarily the embodiment of the polished English gentleman. Of his treatment of social inferiors Dr. Watson records: "Sherlock Holmes was a past master in the art of putting a humble witness at his ease, and very soon, in the privacy of Godfrey Staunton's abandoned room, he had extracted all that the porter had to tell" (CSS, "Missing Three-Quarter," 814). With the distressed women who form so large a part of his clientele, he is, despite his misogyny, courteous and mildly avuncular. In the presence of a bullying villain like Dr. Roylott of "The Speckled Band" Holmes falls back on the English gentleman's traditional resort of impenetrable sang-froid and cutting irony. With an overbearing superior like Neil Gibson in "Thor Bridge" (1922) or the Duke of Holdernesse in "The Priory School" (1904), he is firm and dignified.

One consequence of Holmes's specialist mentality in the early novels was that, as Watson noted, "His ignorance was as remarkable as his knowledge" (CLS, 17). In *A Study in Scarlet* he had never heard of Carlyle or of the Copernican theory of the solar system. By *A Sign of Four* his ignorance of Carlyle had been remedied, and at one point he showed himself the master of a formidably erudite vein of dinner-table conversation: "He spoke on a quick succession of subjects—on miracle plays, on mediaeval pottery, on Stradivarius violins, on the Buddhism of Ceylon, and on the warships of the future—handling each as though he had made a special study of it" (CLS, 227). The *Strand* stories take Holmes's development as a man of culture further. In "The Boscombe Valley Mystery" (1891) he carries a "pocket Petrarch" (CSS, 84) to the scene of the crime and, to relax his mind from more serious matters, turns the conversation to George Meredith (CSS, 90). In later stories he pursues "laborious researches in Early English charters" (CSS, "Three Students," 763), writes a monograph on the polyphonic motets of Orlandus Lassus "said by experts to be the last word upon the subject" (CSS, "Bruce-Partington Plans," 1000), and develops theories about the origin of the "ancient Cornish language" (CSS, "Devil's Foot," 1042).[24]

Holmes's emergence as a rounded man of culture is part of a progressive elaboration of his knowledge and talents which undercuts any sense that he is a specialist in the conventional meaning of the term. By the end of the saga he has shown himself to be expert in the following subjects, among others: tattoos, knots, ears, ciphers, bicycle tires, tobacco ash, newspaper types, perfumes, the development of English script, and names of American gunsmiths. His knowledge of each field has the profundity of the specialist, but its total range is that of the encyclopedist. In this respect Holmes's role is very like that which in "The Bruce-Partington Plans" he ascribes to his brother Mycroft:

> "Well, his position is unique. He has made it for himself. There has never been anything like it before, nor will be again. He has the tidiest and most orderly brain, with the greatest capacity for storing facts, of any man living. The same great powers which I have turned to the detection of crime he has used for this particular business. The conclusions of every department are passed to him, and he is the central exchange, the clearing-house, which makes out the balance. All other men are specialists, but his specialism is omniscience. We will suppose that a Minister needs information as to a point which involves the Navy, India, Canada and the bi-metallic question; he could get his separate advices from various departments upon each, but only Mycroft can focus them all, and say offhand how each factor would affect the other." (CSS, 970–971)

At a time when knowledge was becoming increasingly compartmentalized, this ability to master the various compartments and to range freely between them would have been peculiarly reassuring. Holmes, in fact, was designed to convince contemporaries that one of the traditional roles of gentility—that of the all-round man of knowledge, the liberally educated gentleman—could still survive.

The Holmes of the *Strand* stories becomes more and more the gentleman in his approach to his work. His fascination with the bizarre and his love of abstract scientific puzzles are assimilated into a larger concern for moral and social values. By the time of *The Hound of the Baskervilles* in 1901–1902 he can tell his client, Dr. Mortimer, with quiet pride: "In a modest way I have combated evil" (*CLS*, 295). To the Holmes of the middle period detection is a weapon in the struggle of right against wrong, or rather, since the stories are so deeply imbued with the spirit of gentility, the struggle of honor against scoundrelism.

This change becomes apparent shortly after the beginning of the first *Strand* series in 1891. At the end of his third case, "A Case of Identity" (1891), Holmes expresses his outraged sense of justice in the time-honored manner of the gentleman:

> "The law cannot, as you say, touch you," said Holmes, unlocking and throwing open the door, "yet there never was a man who deserved punishment more. If the young lady has a brother or a friend he ought to lay a whip across your shoulders. By Jove!" he continued, flushing up at the sight of the bitter sneer upon the man's face, "it is not part of my duties to my client, but here's a hunting-crop handy, and I think I shall just treat myself to——" He took two swift steps to the whip, but before he could grasp it there was a wild clatter of steps upon the stairs, the heavy hall door banged, and from the window we could see Mr. James Windibank running at the top of his speed down the road. (*CSS*, 73–74)

Such an outburst and such a threat would have been almost inconceivable on the lips of the cold-blooded scientist of *A Study in Scarlet* or the languorous Decadent of *The Sign of Four*. The early Holmes had little to do with riding whips or invocations to Jove.

This moral zeal and passion for justice complete Holmes's assimilation into the standards of gentility: he is the perfect gentleman hero, the embodiment of the values and aspirations of the contemporary middle-class public. He is also, in a sense, a fantasy version of Doyle himself, whose own life shows a continual aspiration toward perfect gentility. During Doyle's boyhood his mother impressed on him a sense of his family background and its traditions of honor. His historical novels, which he felt to be his finest work, present an idealized picture of a medieval society bound by the codes of honor and chivalry. Throughout his life Doyle remained equally chivalric in his attitude to women. On one occasion he struck his son for describing a woman of their acquaintance as ugly.

"Just remember," he cautioned, ". . . that no woman is ugly."[25] Despite his commitments as a professional writer, he retained a keen interest in public service. His life was punctuated by a series of patriotic gestures: volunteering for active service in the Boer War and writing a pamphlet in defense of the conduct of the English troops, propagandizing the need for England to be prepared against the growth of German military strength, and at the start of the First World War organizing a troop of volunteer Home Guards. A strong sense of *noblesse oblige* made him several times the defender of victims of injustice: he spent large amounts of time and money in passionate and successful fights to reverse the convictions of George Edalji for cattle-maiming and of Oscar Slater for murder, and was among the few who spoke out on behalf of the convicted traitor Sir Roger Casement. When Doyle died, his wife supervised the erection of a tombstone made of British oak bearing the inscription: "Steel True, Blade Straight."[26]

Several of these crusades have fictional counterparts in Holmes's adventures. Where Doyle served his country both by active example and by polemical writing, Holmes becomes involved in counterespionage in a number of the stories—in "The Naval Treaty," "The Second Stain" (1904), "The Bruce-Partington Plans," and "His Last Bow." In "The Bruce-Partington Plans" he approaches the problem of stolen State secrets in a flippant manner, at one point telling Watson to occupy the time by beginning "your narrative of how we saved the State" (*CSS*, 989); but his mission accomplished, he strikes the correctly genteel note of indifference to material reward for his services, though he does accept the gift of an emerald tiepin from "a certain gracious lady in whose interests he had once been fortunate enough to carry out a small commission" (*CSS*, 1000). In "His Last Bow" (1917), which takes place on the eve of the First World War, Holmes speaks in tones of somber patriotism.

Apart from helping to protect his country from external danger, Holmes also defends the interests of the upper middle classes from internal threats. In "Charles Augustus Milverton" (1904) he combats the activities of a blackmailer who specializes in the private follies of the nobility. In general, Holmes presents himself as a suppressor of scandal and an enemy of unfortunate publicity. In "The Missing Three-Quarter" he angrily defends himself against the accusation that he is, by virtue of his profession, a public washer of dirty linen: "Incidentally I may tell you that we are doing the reverse of what you very justly blame, and that we are endeavouring to prevent anything like public exposure of private matters which must necessarily follow when once the case is fairly in the hands of the official police" (CSS, 822).

This aspect of the detective's role would have been especially important to contemporary readers, for during the late Victorian and Edwardian eras the reputation and self-respect of the upper middle classes were badly shaken by a succession of scandals, usually affairs of the gaming table or the divorce court. In several cases—notably the Mordaunt divorce case of 1870, the Aylesford affair of 1876, and the Tranby Croft scandal of 1890–1891—the Prince of Wales himself was involved.[27] It is surely not accidental that the names of these affairs are echoed in those unnarrated cases to which the Holmes stories continually refer. To an age so frequently punctuated by public scandal Holmes, the enemy of the blackmailer and the scandalmonger, would have been a reassuring hero.

Holmes acts as the defender of upper middle-class values in other ways. On a number of occasions he protects clients who are deliberately presented as the epitome of characteristic English virtues. Hilton Cubitt of "The Dancing Men" (1903), whose wife is the victim of attacks by American gangsters, is a romanticized version of Dr. Watson: "He was a fine creature, this man of the old English soil, simple, straight, and gentle, with his great, earnest blue eyes and broad, comely face. His love for his wife and his trust in her shone in his features" (CSS, 615). The most extended handling of this theme occurs in *The Hound of the Baskervilles*, where Sir Henry Baskerville, the heir to the Baskerville estate, is a true chip off the old English block, despite his American upbringing: "He wore a ruddy-tinted tweed suit and had the weather-beaten appearance of one who has spent most of his time in the open air, and yet there was something in his steady eye and the quiet assurance of his bearing which indicated the gentleman" (CLS, 302). The story recounts the struggle to restore the English gentleman to his country estate, a fight in which Sir Henry himself is a passionate helper: "There is no devil in hell, Mr. Holmes, and there is no man upon earth who can prevent me from going to the home of my own people, and you may take that to be my final answer" (CLS, 310). By disposing of the myth of the spectral hound, Holmes is able to lift the family curse and to regenerate the manorial way of life.[28]

Usually, however, the stories present Holmes as a solitary crusader on behalf of the weak and helpless individual. Like his creator, he plays the role of latter-day knight errant. As Pierre Nordon has suggested, he is "one of the last incarnations of chivalry in the literature of the English language."[29] The weak may be the socially powerless, like Jabez Wilson in "The Red-Headed League" or Mary Sutherland in "A Case of Identity," or they may be unprotected foreigners, like the title character in "The Greek Interpreter" (1893) and the Italian couple in "The Red Circle" (1911). All of these characters Holmes helps with a splendid disregard for financial reward.

The chivalric knight is never more knightly nor more chivalric than in his protection of women. On a number of occasions Holmes rescues single women from dangerous situations, and these tales fall into the familiar patterns of sentimental melodrama. "The Copper Beeches" tells the story of a governess working in an isolated country house who provokes the wrath of her employer by prying too deeply into the family secret that he keeps his disobedient daughter locked up in an unoccupied wing of the house. Both the setting and the situation are reminiscent of a stream of Gothic governess fiction which had begun with *Jane Eyre*; Doyle appears to owe a particular debt to Florence Warden's *A House on the Marsh*. In "The Speckled Band" Holmes rescues the heroine from a murder attempt by her stepfather, a situation that had occurred in Miss Braddon's *Charlotte's Inheritance*.

The heroines of these stories are saved from physical harm. On several other occasions Holmes rescues women from sexual danger. In "The Solitary Cyclist" (1904) he manages to prevent a forced marriage. The most extended and lurid handling of the motif occurs in a late story, "The Illustrious Client." The heroine, Violet de Merville, is infatuated with Baron Gruner. As Colonel Sir James Damery explains to Holmes, "It is this daughter, this lovely innocent girl, whom we are endeavouring to save from the clutches of a fiend" (*CSS*, 1092). Gruner, who collects rare china and keeps a record of his past love life in an album, is the epitome of corrupt sexuality, decadent but attractive: "cool as ice, silky voiced and soothing as one of your fashionable consultants, and poisonous as a cobra" (*CSS*, 1096). Holmes approaches the task of rescuing Violet from Gruner with a rare passion, saying: "I was sorry for her, Watson. I thought of her for the moment as I would have thought of a daughter of my own. I am not often eloquent. I use my head, not my heart. But I really did plead with her with all the warmth of words that I could find in my nature" (*CSS*, 1103). The hysterical note that the theme of sexual danger introduces into Doyle's writing reaches a crescendo in the denouement of this adventure: one of Gruner's ex-mistresses, now a fallen woman, throws vitriol in his face.

Whereas Doyle himself crusaded on behalf of Edalji and Slater, Holmes becomes a defender of the unjustly accused: "I am the last court of appeal" (*CSS*, 105), he grandly tells a client in "The Five Orange Pips" (1891). Explaining the nature of his profession in *A Study in Scarlet*, he portrays himself as the man to whom officialdom turns when it is baffled, but in practice he is often the man to whom the private citizen turns when suffering from the wrongs and mistakes of officialdom. In *The Sign of Four* the detective violently disagrees with the police theory that Thaddeus Sholto is the murderer of his brother Bartholomew, although the disagreement is used mainly as an excuse for heavy-handed satire of police blundering, and the question of Sholto's innocence soon fades from the story. When the theme of false accusations recurs in the *Strand* stories—in "The Boscombe Valley Mystery," "The Beryl Coronet" (1892), "The Norwood Builder," and "Thor Bridge"—it is heavily emphasized. At the end of "The Beryl Coronet" Holmes lectures the banker who has harbored and encouraged unjust suspicions of theft against his son, "You owe a very humble apology to that noble lad, your son, who has carried himself in this matter as I should be proud to see my own son do, should I ever chance to have one" (*CSS*, 269). To his role as protector of the weak, Holmes adds that of protector of the individual against the machinelike bureaucracies which society has created. It is a role that Doyle himself played with some passion and intelligence; and as Doyle well knew, it is one which has a perennial attraction in popular literature.

"I am not the law, but I represent justice so far as my feeble powers go" (CSS, 1175), Holmes explains in "The Three Gables" (1926). The distinction is an important one, and Holmes uses his status as private individual rather than public official for more than hushing up delicate scandals and correcting official wrongs. He is in a real sense a law unto himself: the representative of a private code of justice which transcends the technicalities or the inflexibilities of official law. On several occasions Holmes actually breaks the law. In "Charles Augustus Milverton" he and Watson break into the blackmailer's house to steal the contents of his safe. Holmes explains to Watson: "Since it is justifiable, I have only to consider the question of personal risk. Surely a gentleman should not lay much stress upon this when a lady is in most desperate need of his help?" (CSS, 727–728). Watson concurs: "The high object of our mission, the consciousness that it was unselfish and chivalrous, the villainous character of our opponent, all added to the sporting interest of the adventure" (CSS, 731). Holmes undertakes a similar burglary, this time of Gruner's house, in "The Illustrious Client." At the end of the story Watson records: "Sherlock Holmes was threatened with a prosecution for burglary, but when an object is good and a client is sufficiently illustrious, even the rigid British law becomes human and elastic. My friend has not yet stood in the dock" (CSS, 1117).

This private code of justice is to a large extent based on the genteel code of honor, and it can be both harsher and milder than the official law. Holmes feels justified in allowing the thief in "The Blue Carbuncle" to go entirely free, since it is the man's first offense and he seems sufficiently scared to be trusted not to err again. Holmes tells Watson sententiously, "I suppose that I am commuting a felony, but it is just possible that I am saving a soul" (CSS, 172). Although the code allows for such moments of charity, it also sanctions a type of lynch justice against traditional social pariahs. Blackmailers and those who take advantage of helpless women are considered fair game. Holmes stands by without attempting to intervene while Milverton is murdered, and he threatens the villainous stepfather with a horsewhip in "A Case of Identity." After another villainous stepfather, Dr. Roylott of "The Speckled Band," has been poisoned by his own snake, Holmes remarks cheerfully: "Some of the blows of my cane came home, and roused its snakish temper, so that it flew upon the first person it saw. In a way I am no doubt indirectly responsible for Dr. Grimesby Roylott's death, and I cannot say that it is likely to weigh very heavily upon my conscience" (*CSS*, 200–201).

Believing that private revenge is sometimes justified, as he explains to Lestrade when declining to investigate Milverton's murder, Holmes also protects its perpetrators from the police whenever circumstances allow. He merely cautions the murderers in "The Boscombe Valley Mystery" and "The Devil's Foot." The conventions of the genre in which Doyle was writing, however, do not allow such criminals to go entirely free: one suffers from a fatal illness, while the other vows to spend the rest of his life in Africa.

At such moments Holmes steps out of the role of detective and into the role of judge. Several scenes in the stories actually take the form of mock trials. At the end of "The Abbey Grange," Holmes addresses the honest seaman who in a fit of passion has killed the bullying, drunken husband of the woman he loves:

> "See here, Captain Croker, we'll do this in due form of law. You are the prisoner. Watson, you are a British jury, and I never met a man who was more eminently fitted to represent one. I am the judge. Now, gentlemen of the jury, do you find the prisoner guilty or not guilty?"
> "Not guilty, my Lord," said I. (*CSS*, 858)

After a similar "private court-martial" (*CSS*, 777), as Holmes calls it, of a cheating undergraduate in "The Three Students," he subjects the culprit to a bracing moral lecture: "As to you, sir, I trust that a bright future awaits you in Rhodesia. For once you have fallen low. Let us see in the future how high you can rise" (*CSS*, 782).

Such speeches illustrate how much the Holmes of the *Strand* series has transcended the role of mere scientist able to clarify the facts. He occupies a position of almost Olympian superiority from which he can pass judgment on the affairs of men.

This power, which seems like that of the presiding judge in a court, can also take on religious overtones, especially in some of the stories of the later period. In "The Red Circle" Holmes is consulted by a Mrs. Warren who explains that she had heard from a friend of "the way in which you brought light into the darkness. I remembered his words when I was in doubt and darkness myself" (CSS, 947). The language suggests an appeal for spiritual help, and the detective displays appropriate powers of consolation: "Holmes leaned forward and laid his long thin fingers upon the woman's shoulder. He had an almost hypnotic power of soothing when he wished. The scared look faded from her eyes, and her agitated features smoothed into their usual commonplace" (CSS, 948).

The same idea recurs in more pronounced form in "The Veiled Lodger," another of the late tales. The story involves no detection on Holmes's part; he merely goes to hear the confession of the title character to a murder in which she had been an accomplice. Taking down confessions is part of a detective's job, but Holmes's approach to the task is more sacerdotal than legal. He does not inform the police and treats the confession as if its purpose is solely to ease the guilty person's mind. At the end of the interview he divines that the woman is contemplating suicide and offers her philosophical consolation:

> "Your life is not your own," he said. "Keep your hands off it."
> "What use is it to anyone?"
> "How can you tell? The example of patient suffering is in itself the most precious of all lessons to an impatient world." (CSS, 1299–1300)

Like "The Red Circle," "The Veiled Lodger" belongs to the final period of the Holmes saga, a period whose distinguishing feature is a decline in quality. This decline, though marked, is neither total nor entirely uniform. A story like "Thor Bridge," for example, compares favorably with the best of Doyle's work. But on the whole the stories are either weakly plotted or heavily reliant on ideas that had already been better used. That delicate and playful sense of the bizarre which had distinguished Doyle's best work gives way to a cruder sense of the exotic and macabre: the late stories make use of leprosy, rare poisons, Oriental illnesses, rejuvenating drugs, and sea monsters. This desperate search for novel ideas is accompanied by a growing stress on the cruel, the gruesome, and the physically repulsive. In "The Lion's Mane" (1926) there is an almost gloating emphasis on the way the victim meets his death, while the title characters of "The Blanched Soldier" (1926) and "The Veiled Lodger" give lengthy accounts of their experiences in, respectively, a leper colony and a lion's cage.[30]

In keeping with the grossly macabre tone of many of the later stories Holmes becomes a less suave and refined figure: his manners and his wit are at times considerably coarser and more brutal than before. Near the beginning of one of the worst stories, "The Three Gables," he is threatened by a "huge negro," the hired bully of a gang:

He swung a huge knotted lump of a fist under my friend's nose. Holmes examined it with an air of great interest. "Were you born so?" he asked. "Or did it come by degrees?" . . .

"I've wanted to meet you for some time," said Holmes. "I won't ask you to sit down, for I don't like the smell of you, but aren't you Steve Dixie, the bruiser?"

"That's my name, Masser Holmes, and you'll get put through it for sure if you give me any lip."

"It is certainly the last thing you need," said Holmes, staring at our visitor's hideous mouth. (CSS, 1159–1160)

Later in the story Holmes cross-examines a servant whom he has detected listening outside the door by the sound of her asthmatic breathing: "Now, Susan, wheezy people may not live long, you know. It's a wicked thing to tell fibs" (CSS, 1164). He dismisses her with the valedictory: "Good-bye, Susan. Paregoric is the stuff" (CSS, 1165).

The obvious xenophobia of the first passage and the snobbery of the second are both in character, for even at their best the Holmes stories hardly transcend the popular prejudices of their time. But what is new in the late stories is that such prejudices have become harnessed to so crude a conception of comedy. Earlier, Holmes had possessed a dry, effective wit reminiscent of Dr. Johnson. His new vein of repartee, however, aims at being debonair and succeeds merely in being vulgar; it reminds the reader of Sapper's hero, the brutish Bull-dog Drummond. The new humor is used to express not only snobbery and prejudice against blacks but also the anti-German hysteria bred by the first world war. Here is part of Holmes's conversation with Von Bork, a captured German spy, in "His Last Bow":

> "You are a private individual. You have no warrant for my arrest. The whole proceeding is absolutely illegal and outrageous."
> "Absolutely," said Holmes.
> "Kidnapping a German subject."
> "And stealing his private papers."
> "Well, you realize your position, you and your accomplice here. If I were to shout for help as we pass through the village—"
> "My dear sir, if you did anything so foolish you would probably enlarge the too limited titles of our village inns by giving us 'The Dangling Prussian' as a sign-post. The Englishman is a patient creature, but at present his temper is a little inflamed and it would be as well not to try him too far." (CSS, 1085)

This story, originally entitled "The War Service of Sherlock Holmes," sheds light on the falling-off in the portrayal of Holmes. Much of the weakness of the later stories can be attributed to Doyle's growing boredom with both Sherlock Holmes and detective fiction and to his preoccupation with spiritualism—an interest that absorbed most of his time and energy during the last part of his life and which seems incompatible with the writing of tales of ratiocination. Yet it is also clear that, on a deeper level, Sherlock Holmes had by the time of these later tales outlived his proper era.

Holmes was a hero designed for the late Victorian and Edwardian period, and his triumphs reflect the age's belief in certain values: in the power of reason to control the environment and eliminate danger, and in the ability of the gentleman to enforce a sense of justice and fair play. On occasion the stories echo contemporary anxieties, as in their fear of scandal, but in general they express the self-confidence of the period. With their relaxed good humor they participate fully in the mood of what historians have come to call the "Edwardian Garden Party."

This mood and these values were shaken by the impact of the First World War on English culture. In his autobiography Doyle himself speaks of the prelude to the war in these terms: "I can never forget, and our descendants can never imagine, the strange effect upon the mind which was produced by seeing the whole European fabric drifting to the edge of the chasm with absolute uncertainty as to what would happen when it toppled over."[31] This sense of large-scale events beyond the control of the individual, or even of human reason, is the exact opposite of the assumptions on which the Holmes stories were based. "His Last Bow" is thus, as its title implies, a swan song for Holmes and for the world he represents. It is not the final Holmes story—it comes only at the end of the penultimate volume—but it records, metaphorically, Holmes's death.

The mood of the story is bleak and elegiac. This atmosphere contrasts with the earlier stories, where spying and the security of the state had been treated with that light-heartedness which signifies underlying confidence. The threat to England's safety which Holmes had combatted in "The Naval Treaty" or "The Bruce-Partington Plans" belonged to the same level of fantasy as the threat to the honor of the king in "A Scandal in Bohemia." In "His Last Bow" the carefree extravagance which had distinguished the portrayal of Holmes survives only in flashes. He describes his exploits during the years when Watson had thought he was dead with the same panache that had characterized his earlier accounts: "When I say that I started my pilgrimage at Chicago, graduated in an Irish secret society at Buffalo, gave serious trouble to the constabulary at Skibbareen and so eventually caught the eye of a subordinate agent of Von Bork, who recommended me as a likely man, you will realize that the matter was complex" (CSS, 1082). But more characteristic of the story is the concluding dialogue between Holmes and Watson, after the capture of Von Bork, the German agent:

As they turned to the car, Holmes pointed back to the moonlit sea, and shook a thoughtful head.

"There's an east wind coming, Watson."

"I think not, Holmes. It is very warm."

"Good old Watson! You are the one fixed point in a changing age. There's an east wind coming all the same, such a wind as never blew on England yet. It will be cold and bitter, Watson, and a good many of us may wither before its blast. But it's God's own wind none the less, and a cleaner, better, stronger land will lie in the sunshine when the storm has cleared." (*CSS*, 1086)

The balance between grim foreboding and underlying optimism with which Holmes contemplates the prospect of war echoes the attitude Doyle himself later expressed in *Memories and Adventures*. The war, as Doyle describes it, brought personal loss and suffering, but it ended with a reassuring moral: "We did not see the new troubles ahead of us, but at least the old ones were behind. And we had gained an immense reassurance. Britain had not weakened. She was still the Britain of old."[32] In the story Watson, as always, represents the quintessential Englishman: honest, loyal, brave, but not especially intelligent. He remains the same, "the one fixed point in a changing age," and can look forward to the prospect of active service in the coming conflict. Holmes, however, belongs to a more delicate breed: the individualistic and eccentric intellectual rather than the bluff soldier. As he tells Watson, he can only return to retirement after capturing Von Bork; and he implicitly identifies himself with those who may wither before the blast of war.

Doyle revived Holmes in several later stories, collected in *The Case-Book of Sherlock Holmes*, but the insight behind "His Last Bow" is essentially sound. The Holmes of the last volume is a figure adapted to the cruder, tougher mold of the postwar hero. Although later detective fiction abounded in copies of the earlier Holmes, in the fiction of the years immediately following the war he was succeeded by a hero of a very different type, exemplified by John Buchan's Richard Hannay and Sapper's Bull-dog Drummond. These men are like brutalized Dr. Watsons rather than like Sherlock Holmes. They are usually faced with immediate physical danger rather than with intriguing puzzles, and they rely more on physical courage and on fast reflexes than they do on refined speculation. As "His

Last Bow" implies, the war had ushered in a world where figures like Holmes seemed less relevant than they did in the
Edwardian era. In Buchan's *The Three Hostages,* published in
1924, one of the characters explains his dislike of detective fiction to Hannay: "I've another objection to the stuff—it's not
ingenious enough, or rather it doesn't take account of the in-
fernal complexity of life. It might have been all right twenty
years ago, when most people argued and behaved fairly logi-
cally. But they don't nowadays. Have you ever realised, Dick,
the amount of stark craziness that the War has left in the
world?"[33]

NOTES
INDEX

Notes

1. Thief-Taking and Thief-Making

1. Sir Walter Scott, *The Heart of Midlothian*, in *The Waverley Novels*, Dryburgh Edition, VII (Edinburgh, 1893), 163.

2. Patrick Pringle, *The Thief-Takers* (London: Museum Press, 1958), ch. 1 title.

3. Leon Radzinowicz, *A History of English Criminal Law and Its Administration from 1750* (London: Stevens and Sons, 1948–1956), II, 176.

4. *Amelia*, in *The Complete Works of Henry Fielding, Esq.*, ed. William Ernest Henley (London: Heinemann, 1903), VI, 17.

5. Fielding, *Works*, VI, 16.

6. Gilbert Armitage, *The History of the Bow Street Runners, 1729–1829* (London: Wishart, 1932), p. 123.

7. Quoted by Radzinowicz, III, 6.

8. Quoted by Radzinowicz, I, 725.

9. Radzinowicz, II, vii.

10. Radzinowicz, II, 59.

11. Quoted by Radzinowicz, III, 436.

12. "An Inquiry into the Causes of the Late Increase of Robbers, & C.," Fielding, XIII, 106.

13. Quoted by Radzinowicz, II, 147.

14. Quoted in Henry Goddard, *Memoirs of a Bow Street Runner*, ed. Patrick Pringle (New York: William Morrow, n.d.), p. 166n.

15. Quoted by Radzinowicz, II, vii.

16. Patrick Colquhoun, *A Treatise on the Police of the Metropolis*, 5th ed. (London, 1797), p. 196.

17. Radzinowicz, II, 307.

18. Colquhoun, p. 7.

19. Quoted by Radzinowicz, II, 345.

20. Quoted by Radzinowicz, II, 326. For the 1816 conspiracies, see Radzinowicz, II, 333–337.

21. Radzinowicz, II, 338.

22. Pringle, *Thief-Takers*, p. 107.

23. Quoted by Radzinowicz, II, 332.

24. Pringle, *Thief-Takers*, p. 140.

25. Joseph Cox, "Thief-takers, alias Thief-makers," in *Villainy Detected*, ed. Lillian de la Torre (New York: Appleton-Century, 1947), p. 174.

26. Gerald Howson, *Thief-taker General: The Rise and Fall of Jonathan Wild* (London: Hutchinson, 1970), p. 286.

27. "The True and Genuine Account of the Life and Actions of the

Late Jonathan Wild," *The Shakespeare Head Edition of the Novels and Selected Writings of Daniel Defoe, Colonel Jack* (Oxford: Basil Blackwell, 1927), II, 254. Defoe's authorship of this pamphlet, however, is not definitely established.

28. Defoe, p. 259.

29. Howson, p. 311.

30. The translation into modern currency value is given by Howson, p. 86.

31. *The Poetical Works of John Gay*, ed. G. C. Faber (London: Oxford University Press, 1926), p. 488.

32. Howson, p. 115.

33. Howson, p. 6.

34. Defoe, p. 266.

35. *The Poems of Jonathan Swift*, ed. Harold Williams, 2nd ed. (Oxford: Clarendon Press, 1958), III, 1113. The poem has also been attributed to Gay. See Swift, III, 1111–1113.

36. Quoted by Radzinowicz, I, 724.

37. Defoe, p. 274.

38. Defoe, pp. 229, 252, 268.

39. Defoe, pp. 267–268.

40. Major Arthur Griffiths, *Mysteries of Police and Crime* (New York, 1899), II, 424.

41. William Harrison Ainsworth, *Jack Sheppard* (London, 1839), I, 103.

2. Caleb Williams

1. Citations from *Caleb Williams* and the 1832 Preface to *Fleetwood* are to William Godwin, *Caleb Williams,* ed. David McCracken (London: Oxford University Press, 1970).

2. See e.g. Régis Messac, *Le "Detective Novel" et l'Influence de la Pensée Scientifique* (Paris: Librairie Ancienne Honoré Champion, 1929), pp. 178–189; A. E. Murch, *The Development of the Detective Novel,* rev. ed. (London: Peter Owen, 1968), pp. 29–33.

3. "William Godwin," *The Collected Writings of Thomas De Quincey,* ed. David Masson (Edinburgh, 1890; reprint New York: AMS Press, 1968), XI, 330.

4. For the influence of Richardson on Godwin's novel, see Eric Rothstein, "Allusion and Analogy in the Romance of *Caleb Williams,*" *University of Toronto Quarterly* 37 (October 1967): 18–30.

5. Rothstein (pp. 25–26) points out that the parallelism between Caleb's and Falkland's trunks is heightened by their status as the two main articles of evidence against Caleb at his informal trial.

6. *The Enquirer* (Edinburgh, 1823), p. 316.

7. *Oxford English Dictionary,* s.v., "spy."

8. John Groves (himself a spy) reporting a complaint made by Jones, a member of the London Corresponding Society accused mis-

takenly by his fellow members of spying. Quoted by E. P. Thompson, *The Making of the English Working Class* (London: Gollancz, 1963), p. 494.

9. Barbara Hammond and J. L. Hammond, *The Skilled Labourer, 1760–1832* (London: Longmans Green, 1919), p. 375.

10. *A Complete Collection of State Trials,* ed. Thomas Bayly Howell and Thomas Jones Howell, vol. XXIV (London, 1818), p. 709.

11. Quoted by C. Kegan Paul, *William Godwin: His Friends and Contemporaries* (London, 1876), I, 117.

12. William Godwin, *Uncollected Writings (1785–1822),* ed. Jack W. Marken and Burton R. Pollin (Gainesville, Fla.: Scholars' Facsimiles and Reprints, 1968), p. 244.

13. *State Trials,* XXIV, 962–963.

14. Quoted by Erskine, *State Trials,* XXIV, 959. I have been unable, however, to trace the source of this passage.

15. Godwin, *Uncollected Writings,* p. 121. The letter, "No. III. To Sir Archibald Macdonald, Attorney General," was published in the *Morning Chronicle* on March 26, 1793. At this time Godwin was at work on the first volume of *Caleb Williams.*

16. *State Trials,* vol. XXIII (1817), p. 219. The fear of the servant turning spy survived into the nineteenth century. In 1818 a parliamentary committee saw in Jeremy Bentham's idea for a Ministry of Police "a plan which would make every servant of every house a spy on the actions of his master, and all classes of society spies on each other." Quoted by Thompson, p. 82. An unsigned article "Spy Police," published in *Household Words* 1 (Sept. 21, 1850): 611, rejoiced that the Englishman, unlike his Continental neighbors, "can converse familiarly with his guests at his own table without suspecting that the interior of his own liveries consists of a spy."

17. *The Enquirer,* p. 185.

18. *The Enquirer,* p. 182.

19. Numbers 13:16. Rothstein (p. 24) also comments on Caleb's Biblical namesake. However, he interprets the allusion differently: the outcast and powerless figure of Godwin's novel is ironically compared to the Biblical Caleb, who was blessed by God and lived to see the Promised Land.

20. Num. 14:24.

21. Godwin's use of the word "patron" is particularly revealing. David McCracken points out (Godwin, *Caleb Williams,* "A Note on the Text," p. xxv) that in the third edition Godwin changed "master" to "patron" throughout. The latter word carries with it a much stronger reminder of Caleb's obligations to Falkland, and the change would suggest that Godwin was concerned to emphasize this point.

22. Rothstein (pp. 25–26) draws attention to the significance of these incidents. He further points out that the incident of Hawkins' letter is a clear example of how Caleb's conduct offends against Godwin's own social code. In *The Enquirer* (p. 113; quoted by Rothstein,

p. 25) Godwin states that "one of the most sacred principles of social life, is honour, the forebearance that man is entitled to claim from man, that a man of worth would as soon steal my purse or forge a title-deed to my estate, as read the letter he sees lying on my table."

23. Quoted by Erskine, *State Trials*, XXIV, 959.

24. William Godwin, *Enquiry Concerning Political Justice and Its Influence on Morals and Happiness*, ed. F. E. L. Priestley (Toronto: Toronto University Press, 1946), I, xi–xii.

25. *The Enquirer*, p. 188.

3. Vidocq Translated

1. Anon., "Mémoires de Vidocq," *Westminster Review* 11 (July 1829): 162. Citations from Vidocq, his Preface, and the publisher's Introduction are to *Memoirs of Vidocq, Principal Agent of the French Police, until 1827; and Now Proprietor of the Paper Manufactory at St. Mandé*, 4 vols. (London, 1829–1830). This is apparently the second English edition, the first having appeared in 1828–1829. The translator's identity remains in doubt, though the names of William Maginn and George Borrow have been advanced. See Keith Hollingsworth, *The Newgate Novel, 1830–1847: Bulwer, Ainsworth, Dickens and Thackeray* (Detroit: Wayne State University Press, 1963), pp. 239–240n62.

2. J.-M. Quérard, *Les Supercheries Littéraires Dévoilées* (Paris: G.-P. Maisonneuve and Larose, n.d.), III, 945–946.

3. Quérard, III, 945.

4. Régis Messac, *Le "Detective Novel" et l'Influence de la Pensée Scientifique* (Paris: Librairie Ancienne Honoré Champion, 1929), p. 279.

5. Patrick Colquhoun, *A Treatise on the Police of the Metropolis*, 5th ed. (London, 1797), p. 358.

6. *Westminster Review* 11: 162.

7. Anon., "Memoirs of Vidocq," *Literary Gazette*, no. 631 (Feb. 21, 1829): p. 126; Anon., "Memoirs of Vidocq," *Athenaeum*, no. 60 (Dec. 17, 1828): p. 946.

8. "The Memoirs of M. Vidocq," *Spectator* 1 (Nov. 8, 1828): 299; *Literary Gazette*, no. 631, p. 126.

9. For Douglas Jerrold's play, see A. E. Murch, *The Development of the Detective Novel*, rev. ed. (London: Peter Owen, 1968), p. 89. For production details of both plays, see Allardyce Nicoll, *A History of English Drama, 1660–1900*, IV (Cambridge: Cambridge University Press, 1955), 273, 331.

10. Anon., "The Third Volume of Vidocq," *Spectator* 2 (Apr. 18, 1829): 252.

11. Anon., "Memoirs de Vidocq [sic]," *Monthly Review*, n.s. 9 (December 1828): 522, 520.

12. Anon., "Autobiography," *Blackwood's Edinburgh Magazine* 26 (November 1829): 747.

13. The play, first performed at the Britannia Theatre on December 10, 1860, is attributed to Frederick Marchant by Nicoll, V (1959), 764, 849. In the first of these references the production title is given as *Vidocq* and the title on the Lord Chamberlain's manuscript as *The Thieftaker of Paris; or Vidocq*. The version of the title given in my text appears on a playbill advertising the first production, in the possession of the Harvard Theater Collection. The play was never published.

14. For the Runners, see Leon Radzinowicz, *A History of English Criminal Law and Its Administration from 1750*, II (London: Stevens, 1956), 263–269; III (1956), 54–58. The Runners have attracted both bitter attacks, beginning with Dickens' denunciations, and vigorous defense, most notably by Patrick Pringle in his Introduction to Henry Goddard, *Memoirs of a Bow Street Runner* (New York: William Morrow, n.d.), pp. xii–xvi, xxi–xxii. The controversy will be resolved only by further research, but in the meantime Radzinowicz offers a convincing synthesis of the available evidence.

15. Quoted by Radzinowicz, II, 263.

16. Radzinowicz, II, 268.

17. Radzinowicz, II, 263.

18. Gilbert Armitage, *The History of the Bow Street Runners, 1729–1829* (London: Wishart, 1932), p. 263.

19. Sir Walter Scott, *Waverley*, in *The Waverley Novels*, Dryburgh Edition, I (Edinburgh, 1892), 2.

20. Pierce Egan, *Life in London* (London, 1821), p. 10; noted by Hollingsworth, p. 32.

21. *Gentleman's Magazine* 102 (July 1832): 91. For Townshend, see Radzinowicz, II, 266–268; Armitage, pp. 254–256, 264–265.

22. Hollingsworth (p.32n) notes the brief appearance of Townshend, who is not actually named, in Surr's novel. A later fictional portrait of the Runner occurs in James Payn, *Lost Sir Massingberd* (1864).

23. The authorship of *Richmond* has been the subject of disagreement. The *Dictionary of National Biography* (*DNB*) lists it among the works of Thomas Skinner Surr, the author of *Winter in London*. Samuel Halkett and John Laing, in *Dictionary of Anonymous and Pseudonymous English Literature*, ed. James Kennedy, W. A. Smith, and A. F. Johnson, V (Edinburgh: Oliver and Boyd, 1929), 120, ascribe it to Thomas Skinner, Senior (a misprint for Thomas Skinner Surr?) and mention the possibility of Thomas Gaspey's authorship. It is ascribed to Gaspey by William Cushing, *Anonyms: A Dictionary of Revealed Authorship* (Cambridge, 1891), II, 579. The case for Gaspey's authorship is argued on stylistic grounds by Hollingsworth, p. 239n57. Gaspey's *History of George Godfrey* (1828) shows important similarities to *Richmond* in the use of the convention of fictional autobiography, the ironic portrait of the swindles and frauds thriving in London, the penchant for the Gothic and sentimental, and the interest in the

workings of the criminal law. Moreover, according to the *DNB*, Gaspey had earlier held a job on the *Morning Post* which included writing reports of treason trials. This might well have awakened an interest in the Runners and provided a chance to observe their activities, for they were often involved in the turbulent politics of the early nineteenth century. In 1810 they arrested Sir Francis Burdett, and in 1816 they were responsible for the capture of the Cato Street conspirators.

24. *Literary Gazette*, no. 531 (Mar. 24, 1827): p. 181.

25. Hollingsworth (pp. 55, 239n57) complains that the pattern has been continued by historians of detective fiction. Apart from Hollingsworth's useful discussion of the novel (pp. 55–56), the only references to *Richmond* which I have found are John Carter, "Detective Fiction," *New Paths in Book Collecting: Essays by Various Hands*, ed. John Carter (London: Constable, 1934), p. 51n2; Fritz Wölcken, *Der Literarische Mord: Eine Untersuchung über die englische und amerikanische Detektivliteratur* (Nürnberg: Nest, 1953), p. 55; Douglas G. Browne, *The Rise of Scotland Yard: A History of the Metropolitan Police* (London: Harrap, 1956),/p. 74n; Pringle, in Goddard, p. xxx.

26. Anon., "Recent Novels and Tales," *Monthly Review*, n.s. 5 (June 1827): 271.

27. Carter, p. 51n2.

28. All citations from *Richmond* are to *Richmond: or, Scenes in the Life of a Bow Street Officer, Drawn Up from His Private Memoranda*, 3 vols. (London, 1827).

29. Quoted by Robert Cruikshank, *Cruikshank v. The New Police, Showing the Great Utility of that Military Body, Their Employment, & c.*, in *Facetiae: Being a General Collection of the Jeux D'Esprit which Have Been Illustrated by Robert Cruikshank* (London, n.d.), III, 8 (the various pamphlets that compose this volume are paginated separately).

30. Radinowicz, IV (1968), 201.

31. Anon., "The Police and the Thieves," *Quarterly Review* 99 (June 1856): 164.

32. See Margaret Prothero, *The History of the Criminal Investigation Department at Scotland Yard from Earliest Times until To-day* (London: Herbert Jenkins, 1931), pp. 37–38.

33. See Belton Cobb, *The First Detectives and the Early Career of Richard Mayne, Commissioner of Police* (London: Faber, 1957).

34. Cruikshank, p. 32. For the Popay affair, see Radzinowicz, IV, 185–188.

35. Quoted by J. F. Moylan, *Scotland Yard and the Metropolitan Police* (London: G. P. Putnam's Sons, 1929), pp. 152–153.

36. Quoted by Moylan, p. 157.

37. See Cobb, *The First Detectives*.

38. Browne, p. 122.

39. Sir Basil Thomson, *The Story of Scotland Yard* (New York: Doubleday, 1936), p. 120.

40. Quoted by Browne, p. 127. For the Manning case, see Browne, pp. 126–127.

41. See Anon., *Recollections of a Police-Officer, Chambers's Edinburgh Journal,* n.s. 12 (July 28, 1849): 55–59; (Aug. 25, 1849): 115–120; (Nov. 17, 1849): 308–312; 13 (May 18, 1850): 313–318; (June 22, 1850): 387–390; 14 (July 13, 1850): 23–26; (Sept. 28, 1850): 195–199; (Nov. 9, 1850): 294–298; 15 (May 3, 1851): 274–279; 16 (Nov. 15, 1851): 306–311; 17 (Apr. 24, 1852): 259–263; 20 (Sept. 3, 1853): 149–153; "Waters," *Recollections of a Detective Police-Officer* (London, 1856). The 1856 edition includes a final adventure not previously published. Although the *Chambers's* serialization is mentioned in the Preface to the 1856 edition, it is ignored by most bibliographies of detective fiction. It is noted, however, by Eric Osborne in his Preface to the recent facsimile edition of the *Recollections* (London: Covent Garden Press, 1972).

42. See Halkett and Laing, V, 35.

43. Citations from the *Recollections* refer to both the *Chambers's* serialization and the edition of 1856, in that order. Square brackets indicate words added in the 1856 edition, though these textual variations are minimal.

44. "Thomas Waters, An Inspector of the London Detective Corps," *The Recollections of a Policeman* (New York, 1852). This edition omits the two final installments of the *Chambers's* printing but includes several of Dickens' *Household Words* articles on detectives.

45. For foreign translations, see Carter, p. 52n1.

46. Carter, pp. 54–55. Carter's bibliography of the detective reminiscences of the period, though avowedly incomplete, is the largest and most reliable available. See also Michael Sadleir, *Nineteenth-Century Fiction: A Bibliographical Record* (New York: Copley, 1969), II, 33–36.

47. Tom Taylor, *The Ticket-of-Leave Man,* Lacy's Acting Edition, no. 871 (London, n.d.), pp. 9, 55, 57. The term "hawk" was contemporary slang for "detective."

48. Taylor, pp. 51, 42, 49.

4. Charles Dickens

1. Walter C. Phillips, *Dickens, Reade, and Collins, Sensation Novelists: A Study in the Conditions and Theories of Novel Writing in Victorian England,* Columbia University Studies in English and Comparative Literature (New York: Columbia University Press, 1919), 182.

2. Citations from Dickens' fiction, journalism, and letters are to *The Nonesuch Dickens,* ed. Arthur Waugh, Hugh Walpole, Walter Dexter, and Thomas Hatton, 23 vols. (Bloomsbury: Nonesuch Press, 1937–1938). For the fiction, page references are preceded by book number, where necessary, and chapter number, in that order. For the *Letters,* volume and page number are given.

3. For the relation between Wainewright and Jonas Chuzzlewit, see Keith Hollingsworth, *The Newgate Novel, 1830–1847: Bulwer, Ains-*

worth, Dickens, and Thackeray (Detroit: Wayne State University Press, 1963), pp. 185–186.

4. Quoted by Alec W. Brice and K. J. Fielding, "On Murder and Detection: New Articles by Dickens," *Dickens Studies* 5 (May 1969): 47.

5. Dickens' articles are reprinted in, and here quoted from, the volume *Reprinted Pieces* in *The Nonesuch Dickens,* where the two parts of "A Detective Police Party" are combined and retitled "The Detective Police." The articles in *Household Words* by other writers are [W. H. Wills], "The Modern Science of Thief-Taking," 1 (July 13, 1850): 368–372; Anon., "Spy Police," 1 (Sept. 21, 1850): 611–614; [Wills and Dickens], "The Metropolitan Protectives," 3 (Apr. 26, 1851): 97–105; Anon., "Disappearances," 3 (June 7, 1851): 246–250; Anon., "Chips: A Disappearance," 3 (June 21, 1851): 305–306.

6. For the theater incident, see Edgar Johnson, *Charles Dickens: His Tragedy and Triumph* (Boston: Little, Brown, 1952), II, 734.

7. *Letters from Charles Dickens to Angela Burdett-Coutts, 1841–1865,* ed. Edgar Johnson (London: Jonathan Cape, 1953), p. 192.

8. Wills, "Modern Science of Thief-Taking," p. 368.

9. Philip Collins, *Dickens and Crime,* 2nd ed. (London: Macmillan, 1964), p. 213.

10. George Augustus Sala, *Things I Have Seen and People I Have Known* (London, 1894), I, 95; quoted by Collins, p. 196.

11. Humphry House, *The Dickens World* (London: Oxford University Press, 1941), pp. 201–203.

12. Collins, p. 206; see also pp. 213–219.

13. Quoted by Philip Collins, *Dickens and Education* (London: Macmillan, 1963), p. 60.

14. John Forster, *The Life of Charles Dickens* (London, 1872–1874; reprint London: Dent, 1966), II, 69.

15. See e.g. "A Detective in His Vocation," an unsigned article reprinted from the *Bath Chronicle* in the *Times,* Sept. 17, 1853, p. 11: "Mr. Charles Dickens has made much use of Mr. Field's experiences in Inspector Bucket, of the *Bleak House,* and is, we understand, engaged in writing his life." Dickens responded with a denial of both parts of this statement: "amidst all the news in The Times, I found nothing more entirely new to me than these two pieces of intelligence." *Times,* Sept. 18, 1853; reprinted in *Letters,* II, 490.

16. B. B. Valentine, "The Original of Hortense and the Trial of Marcia [sic] Manning for Murder," *Dickensian* 19 (January 1923): 21–22.

17. John Ruskin, "Fiction, Fair and Foul—I," *The Works of John Ruskin,* ed. E. T. Cook and Alexander Wedderburn, XXXIV (London: George Allen, 1908), 272.

18. Edmund Wilson, "Dickens: The Two Scrooges," *The Wound and the Bow: Seven Studies in Literature* (Cambridge: Houghton Mifflin, 1941), p. 36.

19. J. Hillis Miller, *Charles Dickens: The World of His Novels* (Cambridge: Harvard University Press, 1958), pp. 162–163.

20. Morton Dauwen Zabel, Introduction to Dickens, *Bleak House* (Boston: Houghton Mifflin, n.d.), p. xxiii.

21. Miller, p. 168.

22. Miller, p. 171.

23. For Tulkinghorn, see Miller, pp. 172–174.

24. For the change in the characterization of Bucket, see Michael Steig, "The Whitewashing of Inspector Bucket: Origins and Parallels," *Papers of the Michigan Academy of Science, Arts, and Letters* 50 (1965): 575–584.

25. Q. D. Leavis, in F. R. Leavis and Q. D. Leavis, *Dickens the Novelist* (London: Chatto and Windus, 1970), p. 139, notes the separation of Bucket's "everyday good-heartedness from his bloodhound professionalism" and suggests that Bucket is a precursor of the "Split Man" figure represented by Wemmick in *Great Expectations* and Pancks in *Little Dorrit*.

26. For Bucket's lack of understanding in his treatment of the inhabitants of Tom-All-Alone's, see Steig, p. 576; Leavis and Leavis, p. 138.

27. For a somewhat different account of the degree of Bucket's success and failure, see Miller, pp. 175–176.

5. Wilkie Collins and Other Sensation Novelists

1. James Payn, *Lost Sir Massingberd: A Romance of Real Life* (Philadelphia, n.d.), p. 265. The reference is to Inspector Field. I have, however, been able to identify Pollakie.

2. Payn, pp. 268, 270.

3. John Forster, *The Life of Charles Dickens* (London, 1872–1874; reprint London: Dent, 1966), II, 116.

4. Hawley Smart, *At Fault: A Novel* (London, n.d.), pp. 150, 153, 352.

5. *Bleak House*, in *The Nonesuch Dickens*, ed. Arthur Waugh, Hugh Walpole, Walter Dexter, and Thomas Hatton (Bloomsbury: Nonesuch Press, 1938), p. 122.

6. Mrs. Henry Wood, *Mrs. Halliburton's Troubles* (New York, n.d.), p. 127.

7. Mary Elizabeth Braddon (Mrs. Maxwell), *Henry Dunbar: The Story of an Outcast* (London, 1864), III, 40, 193.

8. Braddon, III, 44.

9. Smart, pp. 195, 215.

10. Tom Taylor, *Henry Dunbar: Or, A Daughter's Trial: A Drama in Four Acts: Founded on Miss Braddon's Novel of the Same Name* (London, n.d.), p. 32.

11. Payn, p. 268.

12. Taylor, p. 54. The detective's disbelief in Providence is not an

invariable rule. The original Carter of Miss Braddon's novel remarks, "I'm not much of a church-goer, but I do believe there's a Providence that lies in wait for wicked men, and catches the very cleverest of them when they least expect it" (III, 94).

13. Wood, p. 237.

14. Edmund Wilson, "Why Do People Read Detective Stories?" *Classics and Commercials: A Literary Chronicle of the Forties* (New York: Farrar Straus, 1950), p. 236.

15. For notions of Providence in Victorian melodrama, see Walter C. Phillips, *Dickens, Reade, and Collins, Sensation Novelists: A Study in the Conditions and Theories of Novel Writing in Victorian England*, Columbia University Studies in English and Comparative Literature (New York: Columbia University Press, 1919); T. S. Eliot, "Wilkie Collins and Dickens" (1927), reprinted in *Selected Essays*, 3rd ed. (London: Faber, 1963); T. S. Eliot, Introduction to Wilkie Collins, *The Moonstone* (London: Oxford University Press, 1928).

16. Cf. William H. Marshall, *Wilkie Collins*, Twayne's English Authors Series 94 (New York: Twayne, 1970), pp. 77–85.

17. Citations are to Wilkie Collins, *The Moonstone*, Harper's Illustrated Library Edition (New York, 1898). Because of the plethora of editions of the novel, quotations are identified by section title and (where relevant) chapter number, as well as by page number. The second of Franklin Blake's narratives is distinguished by the addition of the Roman numeral "II."

18. Eliot, Introduction, p. xii.

19. For the Road murder case, see John Rhode (pseud. of Cecil Street), *The Case of Constance Kent*, Famous Trials Series (London: Geoffrey Bles, 1928).

20. Quoted by Rhode, p. 100.

21. For Collins' indebtedness to the case, see Nuel Pharr Davis, *The Life of Wilkie Collins* (Urbana: University of Illinois Press, 1956), pp. 250–252.

22. Patrick Anderson, "Detective Story," *Spectator* 217 (Dec. 23, 1966): 820.

23. For Collins' later experiments with detective themes, see Robert Ashley, *Wilkie Collins* (London: Arthur Barker, 1952), pp. 121–124, 134–135.

24. For police history, see Douglas G. Browne, *The Rise of Scotland Yard: A History of the Metropolitan Police* (London: Harrap, 1956), chs. 12–17. Other useful but more specialized accounts of problems encountered by the police in these years are Belton Cobb, *Critical Years at the Yard: The Career of Frederick Williamson of the Detective Department and the C.I.D.* (London: Faber, 1956); George Dilnot, *The Trial of the Detectives* (London: Geoffrey Bles, 1928).

25. Quoted by Cobb, p. 200.

26. Quoted by J. F. Moylan, *Scotland Yard and the Metropolitan Police* (London: G. P. Putnam's Sons, 1929), p. 160.

27. Sheridan Le Fanu, *Checkmate* (London, 1871), I, 63, 202–203.

28. George Dilnot, *The Story of Scotland Yard* (Boston: Houghton Mifflin, 1927), p. 247.

29. Quoted by Browne, p. 148.

30. Anthony Trollope, *The Eustace Diamonds* (London: Oxford University Press, 1950), II, 88.

31. Quoted by Browne, p. 184.

32. Smart, p. 330.

33. Wilkie Collins, "My Lady's Money: An Episode in the Life of a Young Girl," *"I Say No" or The Love-Letter Answered,* Harper's Illustrated Library Edition (New York, n.d.), pp. 67, 69.

34. Florence Warden (pseud. of Mrs. Florence Alice Price James), *The House on the Marsh: A Romance* (New York, 1884), p. 41.

35. Warden, pp. 218–219.

36. James Payn, *A Confidential Agent* (London, 1881), II, 173.

37. Collins, "My Lady's Money," pp. 70, 68, 71.

38. T. W. Speight, *Under Lock and Key: A Story* (Philadelphia, 1873), p. 119.

39. Braddon, *Charlotte's Inheritance* (New York, n.d.), pp. 328–329.

6. Arthur Conan Doyle

1. Arthur Conan Doyle, *Memories and Adventures* (London: Hodder and Stoughton, 1924), p. 81.

2. Doyle, *Memories,* pp. 74–75.

3. Citations from the Sherlock Holmes novels and stories are to *Sherlock Holmes: A Study in Scarlet; The Sign of Four; The Hound of the Baskervilles; The Valley of Fear; The Complete Long Stories* (London: John Murray, 1929), identified as *CLS,* and to *Sherlock Holmes: His Adventures; Memoirs; Return; His Last Bow and The Case-Book: The Complete Short Stories* (London: John Murray, 1928), identified as *CSS.* Where the context does not make clear from which story or novel a quotation is taken, this detail is supplied in the parenthetical reference.

4. *The Works of Edgar Allan Poe,* ed. Edmund Clarence Stedman and George Edward Woodberry (New York: Colonial Co., 1903), III, 57, 58.

5. Doyle, *Memories,* 74.

6. Poe, *Works,* III, 59.

7. *The Novels and Tales of Robert Louis Stevenson* (New York: Scribner's, 1900), III, 7.

8. See Pierre Nordon, *Conan Doyle,* trans. Francis Partridge (London: John Murray, 1966), p. 228.

9. Richard D. Altick, "Mr. Sherlock Holmes and Dr. Samuel Johnson," in *221B: Studies in Sherlock Holmes by Various Hands,* ed. Vincent Starrett (New York: Macmillan, 1940), pp. 109–128.

10. See Doyle, *Through the Magic Door* (New York: Doubleday, Page, 1915), pp. 51–68.

11. *The Complete Sherlock Holmes*, ed. Christopher Morley (New York: Doubleday, n.d.), p. 869. This Preface is omitted from *CSS*.

12. See Richard D. Altick, *Lives and Letters: A History of Literary Biography in England and America* (New York: Knopf, 1965), pp. 155–163.

13. See Altick, *Lives and Letters*, pp. 233–242.

14. Altick, *Lives and Letters*, p. 82.

15. For Doyle's emphasis on Holmes's knowledge of chemistry and his failure to employ details of contemporary science in the stories, see A. E. Murch, *The Development of the Detective Novel*, rev. ed. (London: Peter Owen, 1968), pp. 182–185.

16. For the supersession of Bertillon's system of anthropometry by the fingerprint system, see Jürgen Thorwald, *The Century of the Detective*, trans. Richard Winston and Clara Winston (New York: Harcourt, Brace and World, 1965), pp. 81–90.

17. T. H. Huxley, *Lay Sermons, Addresses, and Reviews* (New York, 1870), p. 201; noted by Jacques Barzun, "From *Phèdre* to Sherlock Holmes," *The Energies of Art: Studies of Authors Classic and Modern* (New York: Harper, 1956), p. 311.

18. Walter Pater, *Appreciations* (New York: Macmillan, 1901), p. 66.

19. Quoted by Helen Merrell Lynd, *England in the Eighteen-Eighties: Towards a Social Basis for Freedom* (London: Oxford University Press, 1945), p. 82.

20. For a similar view of the novel as a dramatized "struggle of scientific reason against superstition and irrationality" (p. 355), see James Kissane and John M. Kissane, "Sherlock Holmes and the Ritual of Reason," *Nineteenth-Century Fiction* 17 (March 1963): 353–362.

21. For the resemblance between Holmes and the Decadents, see David M. Holmes, "Sherlock Holmes Was a Creature of the Decadence," *Baker Street Journal*, n.s. 15 (June 1965): 103–113.

22. See Doyle, *Memories*, pp. 78–80.

23. Reginald Pound, *Mirror of the Century: The Strand Magazine, 1891–1950* (New York: A. S. Barnes, n.d.), p. 7.

24. For Holmes's knowledge of culture, see Maria von Krebs, " 'Knowledge of Literature—Nil.' Indeed?" *Baker Street Journal*, n.s. 8 (July 1958): 149–157; Clarke Olney, "The Literacy of Sherlock Holmes," *University of Kansas City Review* 22 (March 1956): 176–180.

25. Quoted by John Dickson Carr, *The Life of Sir Arthur Conan Doyle* (London: John Murray, 1949), p. 333.

26. Carr, p. 338.

27. For these cases, see Philip Magnus, *King Edward the Seventh* (London: John Murray, 1964), pp. 107–109, 140–141, 143–149, 222–236.

28. For Holmes's role in "purging the hall of its ancestral blight" in *The Hound of the Baskervilles*, see Kissane and Kissane, pp. 354–355.

29. Nordon, p. 285.

30. For the increased morbidity of the late stories, see Nordon, pp. 241–242.

31. Doyle, *Memories*, p. 331.

32. Doyle, *Memories*, p. 395.

33. John Buchan, *The Three Hostages* (London: Hodder and Stoughton, 1924), p. 15.

Index

Index

Index